MUSINGS OF A WRETCHED SOUL

MAHIMA

Made with ❤ on the Notion Press Platform
www.notionpress.com

Have I betrayed thee, o friend?

"Love is never wasted for it's value does not rest upon reciprocity" - CS Lewis

To embrace emotion, a glorious euphoria. Short lived till it's awakening, renders one helpess. To feel infinitely in grief as though it were a fond memory.

Contents

Contents

Contents

Preface

"Why, my soul, are you downcast? Why so disturbed within me? Put your hope in God, for I will yet praise him, my Savior and my God."– Psalm 42:05. These verses, they pen down the journey of a man tormented by his own suffering. Overwhelmed with the burdens and cares of a world that has but blood to offer. A man of selfish character, ruthless in his pursuits yet aware of the chaos he brings forth. The conflict within - a battle between pleasure and morality, that causes a deep frustration. Abused by love and tormented in pleasure, desperate to seek answers he no longer wishes to find.

These verses, they pen down the journey of a man who found Christ. Amidst his suffering, amidst his sin and guilt, Amidst the pleasures in love and lust he sought desperate in finding meaning. He found Christ. There comes a time when man must confront himself, to accept him for what he has done and to live for what he desires but can achieve it no more. Man comes to this realisation that the world offers him but death and decay. Thus, he squanders his life away in hopes to reach a pinnacle of pleasure be it in the pursuit of love, money and fame. And soon will he come to terms that pleasure treated with greed begets pain and nothing more. There, at that bottomless pit of frustration, guilt and bondage will man find his Savior and his Lord.

Shall these verses offer you, my reader the solace of knowing that you are not beyond redemption, but a creation that was loved from before you were born, a creation that was paid for and bought by the Blood of the Lamb. A creation that has been offered the gift of life. So, rejoice dear reader for thou art not a wretched soul.

Transgression

Home

Thorns piercing my skin as I tread deep,
This unknown land of mystery I seek.
Fortune favors the brave, I hear,
But seldom live to reap the fame.
I remain steady on my feet across this sand,
As I tread forth earnestly to journey's end.
Not far off, I find a hidden hut,
Sheltered beneath the oakwood tree,
Hidden in plain sight, as if only the one
Who sought its existence would find it true.
Smoke rises out of the chimney like a candle,
Put out not far in the past. I smell warmth
Exuding from this hidden Elysium, a mother
Preparing a meal for her children, a father
Holding a child in the safety of his strong arms.
I smell roses and wheat and plenty of fruit,
Warm roasted dinners and leftover pies.
Blinded by my desire for a home, I was veiled.
The thatched roof in flames, I smell smoke.

The flying ash unveils my deluded mind
As I run toward the burning hut, hoping
To salvage what remains, seeking to hold
On to what I could save. Frantic in my motions,
I find a boy gazing through the window.
I scream, wailing in despair, running
Fervently toward the burning cage.
The boy remained at the window,
Unaffected by the burning furnace.
He smiled, as I ran as fast as I could.
He smiled. I could not understand,
My mind still dizzy from the fiery ash.
He smiled; I watched as the fire overwhelmed him,
Crept through his fragile hands and caressed his cheek.
He smiled. I lay weeping on the soft ground,
Helpless in my efforts to save this dear child.
I couldn't reach him in time, as I watched
The hut completely engulfed in its flames.

Rain poured down like a cold embrace
After a cursed summer, I sat drenched,
Watching the pouring rain seep away
The last of the burning embers. I knelt,
Cursing at the clouds, chiding them for their cruel deed,
How reckless in their approach they failed to save
The burning child and his hidden Elysium.
If only they had realized that the smoke
Was not of a kind parent who loved their child,
But a drunk relative seeking to cast agony
Upon a poor child's being. I cried.
My tears lost in the pouring rain, each droplet
Prickling my skin, reminding me of everything
I had failed to protect, failed to care for.
The rain blinded my senses, reminding me
Of a former self, ignorant to the ways of the world,
Living in a hidden bubble, sheltered from the harsh winds,
Deaf to the voices of the screaming wife,
Blind to the pain of the regretful father,
Numb to the lashes upon my back,
Living in a hidden bubble, sheltered beneath
The songs of innocence before I had taken
A bite from the fruit of knowledge, before
I had dipped my feet in the lake of empathy
And drunk from the bosom of greed.
I lay hidden from the cruel ways of the world.

Calm, as the rain faded and my senses renewed,
As the pouring waters washed over my sense of guilt,
Restored from a tranquil epiphany of yonder day,
I lay beneath the oakwood tree, polishing
A stone to carve out an epitaph for the lost soul.
This child unknown to the civilized world, this child
Unknown to the conniving thorns of vengeful mockers.
I etch, "a fleeting soul, an immortal smile."
As I dig through the hard ground, I smell
The soft essence of the earth, soil underneath
My tardy nails, as my sweat trickled down my brow,
Watering the soiled ground. To lay
The resting corpse of the boy who lived beneath
The oakwood tree. I cry as I give his fragile,
Burnt corpse back to the earth. Memories of a past self
Come afloat, a time of agony, a time of remorse.
I felt my senses crumble, a coffin as brown
As freshly ground coffee, held the one I loved
Closer to my heart than mine own soul.
I bled verses for her eulogy but to no avail.
My heart beat tirelessly, hoping to wait
Out that agony, but it never understood.
Grief never ends, and scars never heal.
A leaf falls upon my brow, calming my senses,
As I pile upon sand to cement the departed.

As I lean upon the majestic oakwood's trunk,
I begin to recollect the boy's smile, I ponder.
Had he never experienced suffering which led
Him ignorant to his surrounding or was suffering
All he ever knew? I did not know this boy,
But everything I felt was embedded to his being.
Does a parent teach a child to stay away from the flame,
Or does the child seek to learn on its own?
Does misery invite its company or is the company
Enamored by misery? These conflicting thoughts
Peruse my being as I lay restless beneath
The majestic oakwood tree. I rest.
A bright light envelops me whole.
For a moment, I experience everlasting rapture.
The boy, clothed in robes whiter than snow,
Adorned with gemstones glistening rays of light.
He spoke, "I thank you wanderer,
I heard your cries, I saw you run,
I felt your love far beyond the fiery ashes."
A chariot awaited with my name carved
On the pedestal. I ask, "where would this take me?"
The boy replied, "the home you were searching for,
Your journey's end, your final reward."
I waiver for a moment, seeking to find solid ground
An end? To all this suffering?
I hesitate, I muster up the courage to say,
"Fortune Favors the brave and I am but
A coward, rest well boy beneath

the oakwood Tree for my time is yet to come,
I found solace beneath the majestic trunk
And I am yet to experience it whole."
"Wise beyond measure, dear wanderer
Take heart, for to love is for the brave
And to grieve is for the warrior."
A prickling feeling rushes through my cheek
As I felt the sun shine brightly upon my brow
I smile, for I find the oakwood tree sheltering
My brow and calming my soul, I smile
For I was perceived, appreciated and rewarded
I smile, for I am yet to live beyond this life of misery
I smile, for I shall love once more, I rise.

An Encounter with Winter

I lay awake as I peer into the night sky;
A certain dream rendered my pain unending,
A high fever and breathless wandering,
Calls upon my mood as steady as my trembling arms.
An eerie shadow cast over mine eyes,
As I stare at an epitaph containing no high praise;
A soulless grave with a ragged coffin.
A life of regrets lay calmly beneath the concrete.
Mirthless aura filled the milieu,
As the green faded round the grave,
And winter creeps forth like a bloodthirsty wretch;
Ensuing her visions of calamity spread.
Death and decay all around me,
As I feel her fingers caress the last green maple leaf.
Her hounds of tyranny carry her feet,
As she rides on their back for her encounter with me.
Her cold eyes reflect mine own.
I hear her heart beat faint and near,
A beat of sombre rhyme, a dying soul.
I feel her close as she whispers slow,
"A life of regrets or a lifeless soul."
I gaze at her face with curious animosity,
Watch her shed red on a canvas as white;
I see no villain but a painful sight.
I gaze again but now with pity,

A lifeless soul what once could've been.
Forced upon her head an eternity of suffering,
Tormented by her deeds, a murder within.
I place my hand caressing her cheek,
And wipe her tear wallowing in grief.
The red smudged further on the snow-white canvas;
A portrait so beautifully painful it wrecked me whole.
I peer back into my unmarked grave,
"A life of regrets or a lifeless soul?"
She gasps for air as her tears well up;
Her want for companionship laid me bare.
Two of a kind, our souls would mingle,
Lifeless souls, an eternity and chaos.
I rest my hand to my side,
As she begs me to hold her close.
Her sweet beckoning still echoing in my ears;
I turn around from her to my unmarked grave.
As I gaze back into her eyes one last time,
A majestic sight of what could have been.
But I now realize as I feel my heart beat,
A life of regrets is still worth living.
And I bid you farewell, my sweet lady Death,
Till we meet tomorrow day.

Burden

A hypocrite run amuck, a tired soul.
Tearing apart limb from limb.
What once was a childlike glow,
Yet what remains at present,
A hollow shell of a broken man,
Torn apart by fangs of poison,
Seated deep within his lungs,
Suffocating him from within,
Like a snake that slithers forth,
Masked as wise company,
Clenches your throat from afar.
Broken bones and a voice now
Hidden from the world, a life
Drowning in its own filth,
A mockery of creation itself.
This being separated so far from
Its original self, a work of decay
And ruin sprung forth from evil.
Lay rotten on this dark green earth,
Waiting its end and writhing in pain,
But it shall neither rest nor cease to
Exist, and that is its burden to bear.

Mirrors

Shattered mirrors across the room,
Reflections born of a sinful soul.
What once was no longer in sight,
A cruel face masked in sympathy.
Yet these mirrors reflect not his
Kindness but his wrath in excess.
No amount of kind words nor
Caring acts could wash away his sin.
Red painted in his cheek; a story hidden.
Shattered mirrors across the room.
He finds himself in corners shedding
More red bruises from his palms.
Shards of glass stuck deep under his vein,
Bleeding yet numb to the pain.
He carries himself back to the mirrors,
To find once again, hoping to see a change
In his skin yet all he found were the
Reflections born of a sinful soul,
Blemished in all its glory,
In defiance to his former self.

Wanderer

A wanderer with no place to call home,
restless in his pursuit to find meaning,
wanders through broken palaces,
hoping to find rest in such lofty rooms.
He hopes to find a home in every touch,
every conversation, and every lie,
lies he hears dearly from people around,
hoping that one day they might pity him
and avail him with the truth, the truth
of their wretchedness and heartache,
the truth of their own pursuit to find
meaning and the throats they stepped
on to find pleasure in their lives.
He craves only to be invited to a table
wherein snakes reside and poison served.
What desperation in want of such carnage,
to die is no more a watchful option.
Thus he finds himself in places without
life or joy nor love or compassion,
a life of pleasure and meaningless torment,
endless as days pass by and minutes fade.
Yet he reminds himself to be with company
doth better than being by his lonesome,
for what good a man who lost everything
to journey by himself and lose more

than to stay in the presence of cowards
and haughty fools to use and discard,
justified in his attempts to find rational
in his pursuits of overcoming abandon,
yet he finds himself all the more lonesome,
the table filled with snakes now seem
a distant view, he fears for himself waiting
for a neighbor to pierce his skin with fangs
and drink the wine of lust and vengeance
in pursuit of overcoming abandon and
worrisome about losing more of everything.
Dear wanderer, "thou hath lost thyself."

Grief

A wave rushing through my senses,
Submerged my entire being,
A weighted feeling on my chest,
Lungs filled with blood, I suffocate.
My heart beats tirelessly,
Hoping to wait out this agony,
But it never understood:
Grief never ends,
Grief never ends.

Hatred

I am the vassal of mine own hatred,
Singing songs of woe to those that come near.
Her eyes blinded by pain and weariness,
As they wander across, seeking to find;
Remnants of love in mine vessel of hate.

Desperate in hoping that my treasure of goodness,
Lay deep within and thus seeking to hold on—
To this thorny plant, she dug her hands deeper.
Spilling blood over mine vessel, deeper and deeper—
She clawed, suffocating in her quest to find goodness.
Her lungs screamed in panic,
As she felt herself drowning in her own blood,
An ache in her heart as she plunged deeper.

Seeking more desperate in hope,
Of a light within the darkness,
Yet as she swam deeper and deeper;
Came nothing forth but more darkness.

In pursuit of finding goodness in kind,
She suffocates and suffocates still,
She has found nothing.

In pursuit of redemption,
I have become hate,
I have become all of it and more,
I am nothing.

Angel of Death

The lights be damned
as darkness ensues,
Shall the night lay silent
and the demons pursue.
Screams of pain
and agony abound,
Hurt my kindred soul
and burn me down.

The night still silent
and woe unto you,
Wretched mortal
in pathetic blue.
Sadness and sorrow,
a third shall come,
Grief shall he be called,
this tyrant shall pursue.

And darkness still lay,
lie still and keep silent,
As the night does so,
might grief pass you by.
And leave you alone,

so shall you wait,
Till morning's rise forth
and hear of a killing,
In the neighbor's barn door.

Grief takes its vengeance
lest you lay silent,
Count your blessings
and live it well,
For the night shall appear
and darkness will return,
And grief shall he enter
with a knock on your door.

Lie still and keep silent,
pray he may pass you by,
And a neighbor to attend
for grief's a stranger,
you've known him since forever.

Patient Grave

As time moves slow and seasons change,
As the rain falls hard and summer veils,
As the clouds move slow and autumn arrives,
As days grow short and winter takes root,
As grass turns green and spring bursts forth.

I lay still, patiently waiting for a change,
Basking in the warmth of the sunlight,
Taking shelter from the pouring rain,
Beneath the maple tree soon turn grey,
Waiting still by the firewood for the night,
Waking early by the greener paths I find.

Seasons pass and time marches forth,
Waiting patiently for a hope that lives on,
My hair turns gray and I feel my legs weaken,
For this mortal torment my heart deemed worthy,
Patient in suffering, patient in strife,
As time moves on, I lay down quiet.

Days pass and I look to the clouds,
Moving slow but never still in its path,
Where do they go? What awaits them?
Do they find peace? Do they find relief?
Do they break apart and pour down in agony?
Or do they find their way to heaven in all its glory?

I lay still, patiently waiting for a change,
As the ground beneath me gives way,
I look down to see an iron casket,
"Lay here patiently" read my epitaph,
As I stepped down to take my place,
I found it, that precious thing.

Fortune

Broken Shells

A distant memory, a past forgotten,
What ecstasy let run wild?
Visions of Jericho tumbling down,
Ravaged castles and empty streets,
A king without a crown,
A castle without its subjects,
And a kingdom without its queen.
What ecstasy should cause such chaos?
What pleasure worth this pain?
An empty nest with broken shells,
A sober reminder of what once was.
These broken shells spin a story,
Of a soul struggling within.
Time passes as it matures in length,
Time passes when it tears apart.
What once cared for it with such warmth,
Leaving behind these broken shells.
A sober reminder of what once was.
Set free your dreadful heart,
Let it soar a thousand miles,
Find it broken on the dirt, a memory.
That past forgotten, a haunting present.
Gather the pieces and soothe it with care,
Let it heal and renew in a fountain of warmth.
Speak unto its being whispers of love,

And soon shall it soar so high above.
This kingdom once again without its queen,
This broken crown a thorn to adorn.
This empty castle now filled with a memory,
A fountain of warmth, a dwelling abode.
Lest this cycle, a memory remain,
A past forgotten, the kingdom awaits.
For its queen shall return a yonder day.
What ecstasy let run wild then?
This empty nest shall be whole again.

Love

I feel so elated, a warm blanket
Covering me with this overwhelming
Sense of joy and happiness.
I'm beginning to yearn for this feeling
To realize that someone out there
Wishes for me deeply.
Oh, love, I really do care about you.
Talking to you has made me feel happy,
This abundance of joy, an ecstasy.
I feel eerie, as if it isn't a part of me.
I could never experience this exhilaration.
But with you, my love, I begin
To feel everlasting rapture.
I don't want to sleep now
Or wake depressed.
My desire to want
To cuddle and nurse this overflowing cup.
A river of happiness and peace.
Nothing else matters to me,
Not life nor death.
I wish to stay here in this moment
Forever. But time moves on,
And sooner than later I have to accept
That this feeling of elation
Was nothing more than a fleeting moment.

Fear

I fear the vast dimensions of eternity,
I fear the anguish that comes from rejection,
The sorrow that comes through betrayal,
The pain that moves through loss.
I fear the ones closest to me
More than murderers and thieves,
This paranoia beyond repair,
This heart of mine beyond salvation.
The thought of loving someone
A distant memory, the fear of losing
A cherished one overshadows
The joyful memories that existed.
The fear of betrayal by a loved one
Overweighs the glee of trust.
The fear of being rejected by a friend
Overwhelms the hopes of companionship.
The fear of never-ending agony
Massacres the joy of living.

A Letter

So deep the ocean blue,
So great is my love for you;
A Never-ending ripple in time,
I wish you were forever mine;
A solace in the depths of space,
A hug or a warm embrace;
Is all I need to feel eternal joy,
My Achilles heel in the battle of Troy,
Such wondrous beauty,
such marvelous grace,
An angel's kiss is all it takes;
To seal this bond caste by fate.
A mortal realm, a dying soul,
So full of love I can't withhold;
Such speechless passion, a calming wind,
So full of love I can't rescind;
These final words may forever tell,
My love for you that never fell.

Ocean Deep

We both fell, knowing
we'd never be the same again.
We were madly in love,
Not knowing what love actually meant.
We flew through the sky,
Knowing we could never come down,
To the moon and never back wasn't a gift;
It was a curse.

We both fell into the ocean.
I then realized that while I drowned in the depths,
You swam through the shallow waters.
While I was gasping for breath,
You felt the warmth of the ocean.
While I emptied my lungs trying to reach you again,
You enjoyed the perfect view from the shores.
While I desperately clung on to the hope
That you'd reach out and save me,
You were too busy building sandcastles and finding seashells.

I realized then how treacherous the fall was,
How I had plunged myself deep into endless emotion,
While you still held on to a floating piece of wood
Because you were too afraid to let go.

I'll still wait for you,
At the bottom of the ocean where my heart
Still beats for you and you alone,
With my arms outstretched,
Hoping you'd embrace me when you finally choose to fall,
My mind wishing and praying you'd understand
How lonely it felt at the deep end
With no one to hold your hand and tell you that it's okay.

My body still lingers to feel your warmth,
To share the depths of the ocean with you,
To show you how truly beautiful the ocean really is,
If you'd just dive in because my hand
Will hold you through it all.

I'll still wait for you in the depths of the ocean,
The ocean I call love.

A Lover's Quarrel

I was always there,
Standing in the shadows,
Waiting for you;
Sitting through lonely nights,
Dreaming about you;
Running across deserted roads,
Searching for you;
All those sleepless nights,
All those rainy days,
All those empty spaces,
I realized I was only trying
to fill the void in my heart.
You weren't the right part of my puzzle,
I just wanted you to be.
The missing piece, The lost ring,
The fallen petal, But the heart wants
what it wants. I will always be there,
That never fading shadow
in the scorching sun, that drop
of moonlight in the cold chilly evening,
That place you call home
on this plane of uncertainty.

Pearls

As precious as the pearls beneath the sea,
Nursing back to health my heart did she.
Understanding and kind, the words she doth speak,
Slow to love but trust she doth seek.
Ravaging beauty, a sight to behold,
Engorged in life, a helping hand she'd never withhold.
Easy on the eyes, a fair maiden she doth is,
Not a single waste of breath and bliss.
Assuredly so, her love is grand,
Infinite as the grain of desert sand.
Rest easy, my love of past history,
Kind a soul like yours to come across a mystery.
Joy and peace I hope find you eternally,
This poem I end with a smile gratefully.

A Forever

When it ends,
When the smiles fade away,
When the darkness starts creeping in,
When the laughter dies away,
When the walls start closing in,
When the mirrors shatter around you
And ceiling starts dripping with blood,
When fear crawls up your spine
Like a centipede and the loneliness
Pierces your heart like a rusted dagger,
Slowly and painfully, when the liquid
You try to ingest is corrupted with agony
And suffering, when you wander about
Consuming the aroma of self-hatred
And misery. You'll find me, a candle

Shimmering in the corner of the room,
A lonely star in the moonless sky,
A street lantern in the darkest of alleys,
A firefly in the deepest jungle,
You'll find me. A helping hand,

A desperate embrace, the warmth of a fireplace
In the coldest of nights, the gentle touch
Of a cool breeze in the heat of summer,
You'll find me. A promise kept,

A vow undead, a bond never forgotten,
And a love that never fell.

Fleeting

Amare

Lotus white, a calming breeze,
Aphrodite's beauty could not compare.
Kind eyes, it melts my heart,
Seraphim's child from heaven depart.
History speaketh of marvellous beauty.
Mine own eyes doth find such a tale,
Irresistible as I lay in awe of her graceful deity.
Rest assured my speechless soul, her heart of Midas' gold.
Await my heart, rush not your heaved beating.
Melt thine ego and find thine seating,
Arthur's table, a knight in waiting.
Seldom utter your fanciful desire,
Wait in patience, find your peace.
Amare, sweet maiden, mine eyes still centered,
Myths of destiny I rave on in pursuit.
Icarus' fall, I find myself admiring thee but only from afar.

Vivaldi's Letter

A concerto so lovely, so euphoric,
A movement of such magnitude and splendour.
This tapestry of divine colours,
Such daintiful grace, such marvellous beauty.
Eyes shone like moonlight glistening,
Glimpses of a faint smile so luminous,
A pedestal of never-ending admiration.
Allegro non molto, a winter's heart,
A crevasse in a frozen ocean.
Shades of yellow oozed over a bloodied canvas,
Like the ray of sunshine creeping through rose windows,
Illuminating with a melody so warm.
Presto, a summer's bloom,
Melting ice and vanishing darkness.

Rose Gold

Shades of pink with a heart of gold,
Imagine her a midnight rose,
Locks of ivy, her poison divine.
Locks of vanilla, her essence angelic.

Such fair skin, such arduous beauty,
Lay by her side, a calming residence.
A graceful touch, a deity enchanting,
I turn to poesy upon her gaze.

A gaze so deep, the ocean blue,
Coffee-scented eyes, a cup filled
With such warmth to bequeath,
A remedy for this broken shell.

Beneath her autumn eyes, a lair.
Forbidden to the common man,
A lair of unbridled compassion,
Awaits its seeker, a treasure trove.

Treasures filled with love and care,
Moulded from ages of torment,
Ages of pain and misery abide,
Love purified in a forlorn furnace.

Caution, I pray you tread mildly,
This treasure, a pure heart require.
Let thine mind seek to care
Beyond her beauty, her love repair.

These lines I pen down unworthy,
Her ambrosial smile an eternal flame,
This dying candle set ablaze,
Sent Icarus to find a higher state.

Love eternal, her heart of gold,
Rosy cheeks a dear shade of pink,
Verses tenfold could not compare,
Her life a fairy tale, seeker beware.

A Ride

As I drive through the night, abandoned,
flashes of lights escape mine eyes.
A heaviness upon my shoulders,
I grip the wheel with a numbing arm.
As I weave through the motions,
the worrying sight of endless roads,
a tiring dizziness felt upon my brow,
as I hold on fervently to the wheel,
desperate in search of control,
reckless in mine hope for purpose.
I speed through the darker gray,
flashes of light escape mine eyes,
an eerie feeling in a rear-view mirror.
I see mine reflection chasing after,
a reality I'd spent eons fleeing from,
restless in its attempt to find me.
Glimpses I find in the passenger's seat,
her eyes still glistening from back when
we raced through the interstate,
seldom grieving for things unknown.
I blink and I find her again but now,
bloodshed! Red dripping from her brow,
and she looks back into mine eyes,
bloodied clothing and a broken arm.
She whispers, "slow down, Mon Cheri."

Tears welling in mine eyes, I stop,
this reckless abandon no more.
I release my hands from the wheel,
a weight lifted from mine shoulders.
I rest for a minute to mourn her loss
and find joy in acceptance of reality.
I drive.

Confession

Chai

a familiar feeling in a foreign town,
cup of chai but it doesn't warm you down.
lonely people in crowded places,
I try to remember but all I see are foreign faces.

songs that remind me of a place called home,
that drive up the highway the roads I'd roam.
chai that was warm, the burn on my tongue,
wake up dear fool, the alarm bells rung.

these blaring noises and lit up towers,
I hear nothing and I see as darkness empowers.
the silent commute but all I hear is wailing,
with each passing day I see these people fading.

the feel of the car as I pulled up around the block,
the barks of the street dogs as the evening grew dark.
the pleasant smell of my mother's cooking,
as I'd stare out my window at the crescent moon I'm looking.

intense traffic, a whirlwind of horns,
walking ahead I find these people are but pawns.
disgruntled faces and unpleasant mornings,
as I walk on ahead heeding not their warnings.

the Chai my mother brings me,
the warmth of the cup it fills me with glee.
I wonder when I'd see her again,
to fall asleep in her arms and dream again.

A Mother's Light

A cursed blessing far beyond escape,
Mortal ties far beyond love and affection.
As she lays still in the middle of the night,
Watching her children sway to the sounds
Echoing from the stars, a ladder shines forth;
Illuminating her bedroom with divine lanterns.
Come forth angels of serenity and grace,
To shed warmth and kindness for Her's sake.
They come to bear witness to a strength;
Far Greater than Achilles yet no mortal flaw.
Her heart beat sirens the drums of chaos
Yet her soul clings to peace and forbearance.
She is found alone with neither a guardian,
Nor a nurse to guide her gently through the night;
But this light, one that shines through the darkness.
One that breaks mortal conflict and puts an end
To wars beyond our imagination, that light.
That light shall guide her and be with her,
Till tomorrow come and she shall bear witness
To her offspring about that light, she carries
With her to comfort her through this journey
Of life and be with her till kingdom come.

Mother do thou art know

Her palm I touch, my mind weakens slow,
My numbness fades as tears stain mine cheek.
These hands that nurtured and cared for me,
These hands they brushed mine hair for me.
Mother, do thou art know how I care for thee.

Like a river breaketh through dams overboard,
Love I have too afraid to voice it, hurts my soul,
Renders me unable to move or uphold,
This solemn exterior I find it unraveled.
Mother, do thou art know how I care for thee.

My heart it breaks each moment I gaze
Upon your beauty, your matchless grace.
She calls me by mine own wretched name,
Yet in her voice, it speaks of a knight.
Mother, do thou art know how I care for thee.

This knight she birthed and hopes in still,
My tears they well yet caution stills,
This hardened heart of mine I yet despise,
Hope to voice a cry or rather a plea suffice.
Mother, do thou art know how I care for thee.

Patient in suffering her love abounds,
She knows no bearing of pride nor lust.
Her heart of love that causeth her pain,
Yet she sustains to love still and more to gain.
Mother, do thou art know how I care for thee.

I gaze upon her as she makes her bed,
Her tired self still marching forth,
An aching back and weakened bones,
A piece of what once was whole.
Mother, do thou art know how I care for thee.

Her eyes they gleam at wonders so small,
In her eyes, I find a little girl who crawls,
So full of life and passions abound,
Her desires to satisfy my heart announce.
Mother, do thou art know how I care for thee.

This hope shall renew in mortal embrace,
To find her peace and joy these wretched days,
My one true claim to redeem myself,
To find her well and true in her own self.
Mother, do thou art know how I care for thee.

Whence she find herself in that little girl,
Whose dreams were left unforgotten,
Fulfilled and loved till ages past,
Shall I then turn to her and speak,
"Mother, do thou art know how I care for thee."

Remnant

A Portrait

If I could paint a portrait about how I feel,
it'd show you brush strokes of infinite warmth.
The shade of brown when the sun meets your eyes
reminds me of hot cocoa on a rainy afternoon—
the sweet essence of chocolate renders a familiar feeling,
as when your eyes meet mine.

Pondering thoughts of intimacy and shades of blue—
the kind of blue I find beyond the shores,
the kind of blue I find in Van Gogh's portraits of woe.
Lilacs coloured purple,
the idea of royalty I find in your aura,
so unafraid to be yourself,
enchanting in everything you do.

Red I find in custom roses, and red I find gauded rubies,
red that matches this beating heart,
and red that spills over a glass of wine.
Sunflower fields shown with yellow,
the assured ease that fills my heart
when I lay next to you,
like a warm fireplace fuelled by embers
glowing fiercely with such yellow.

Grass, I find near the lakeside; green I find well-watered,
evergreen showers of laughter and care—
you are everything mother nature seldom shares.
Pink, I hold dearest to my heart,
the pink I find in your careless blush,
a pink that washes away the dark—
care to stay and mend my heart.

This portrait I'd paint for a million years,
using colours beyond one's hopeless contrivance.
But it could never inch close
to portraying such magnitude,
such reverence, such grace, and such love.

Time Passes

Past autumn, when I bathed in your embrace, Seeking solace
in the midst of your warm hands,
Rosy cheeks filled with such warmth and comfort —
Kissing them would heal this numbing self.

Fingers intertwined till death do us part,
That calm embrace I held dear to my soul,
Glancing at each other, standing but an arm's length,
Wishing that forever and nothing less.

Unspoken vows of trust and unbreakable faith,
A smile that could light a burnt-out candle within,
That burning passion I hoped would last for eternity —
Everything I felt unbelievably impassioned.

The ides of March wherein I am found alone,
My hands empty, clawing at the walls for comfort,
Writhing in pain, my lips dripping with blood —
Summer, you blasphemous hypocrite.

My heart turns to stone as once deeply feared,
I find comfort lying against the broken glass,
The rays of light piercing through the broken window —
Summer, you leave nothing but ashes.

My fingers soiled in the mud, digging my own grave,
This chaotic mind desperate for nothingness,
I scream in agony, left without care —
Summer, you stole everything from me.

Blinding Oath

When the years pass by,
And the night grows old,
When tears lay dry,
And the heart gets cold.

Remember my vow,
A promise still kept,
Rest easy my love,
This comfort accept.

Fortune favors the brave,
The meek need it more,
Unashamed to crave,
Sand by the sea shore.

Infinite to the naked eye,
Such is my want,
To pray that this goodbye,
Will forever my soul haunt.

Enchanting

A quiet darkness in these enchanting woods,
The silence of the trees, this chilling aura.
The sounds of crickets and birds singing
Seem but a distant memory in these hollowed woods,
Perched on top an oakwood branch, the owl rested,
Gazing upon the two lovers beneath the tree.

Whispers of love screamed in excess,
Craving each other's company and nothing less.
Laughter and warmth filled the milieu,
What once was empty now filled to the brim.
This cup of wine so inviting and tasteful,
Drunk on love and pleasure everlasting.

Moonlight seeps through the canopy,
Illuminating the present and their desires.
Lips so tender glistened upon by the light,
Hands rested, caressing the cheek.
Eyes trembling upon gazing at each other,
This eternal embrace, such glory and such praise.

A broken twig, a branch stepped on,
Alarmed the owl perched upon the branch.
An embrace ceased as the night grew old,
The sounds of crickets echo once again.
The lovers unaware of what was to come,
Frightened as they let go, a broken twig.

The darkest hour warning its company,
The woods seemed a maze, a path forgotten.
Lost in their passion, a reality misplaced,
No such ecstasy or eternal moonlight.
This fleeting hour set upon its course,
And morning brings forth an end to this union.

This setting hour led to a frantic prayer,
The boy looked up to the melting night sky.
He then wished upon a dying star,
A wish of luxury, a wish of hope,
That this night would embrace the three.
"This Love, Mon Cherie and I," said he.

Broken Savior

Reminiscence of an ideal dream,
Fills mine heart to the brim,
Wishful dreams and earnest prayer,
Watch me drown slowly,
As I plunge deep to save her.

My lungs filled with water,
As I flee deeper into the waves,
This place of darkness and wrath,
What once was my home,
Now my destiny to bring her back.

As the water blinds my senses,
This feeling all too familiar,
My wretched past a distant memory,
My saving grace I pray you wait,
To save thee from this woeful fate.

I am not your savior, I know this well,
White knight unblemished I wish it were true,
I am but a broken man wounded by my ways,
Take my hand nonetheless Mon Cherie,
I'll keep you safe in these broken walls.

Infinite

We are inevitable, you and I,
As the high mountains perish,
And the oceans breathe their last drop.
As the trees quit their melody, and their leaves depart,
Flowers laid trampled on the sand, and roses left unhanded.
As the birds lay weary, and the bison bellows no more,
As the children lay dazed, this world collapsing on its own.

We are inevitable, you and I,
Our love soars higher than the cliffs could imagine.
Our love runs deeper than the ocean's soft bed,
Roots intertwined, majestic in our stature.
We stand tall, flourishing flowers of violets and azure,
Melodies richer than the nightingale's sacrifice.
As the children lay dazed, this love abounding.

We are inevitable, you and I.
No mountain too high, no ocean too deep.
The trees shall sing our melodies and their roses.
I shall grant you dearly, a sanctuary of flowers.
The birds shall soar to remember our love, and the bison

Shall bellow to remember our vows.
The children gushing with joy as the world gives way.
This love shall grow, for you and I are infinite.

Rusted Blade

I gaze lovingly upon her kind eyes,
As she drives the rusted blade
Deeper into my soul, I smile knowing
I'd perish at the hands of my lover.
She'd look into my eyes and watch me
Bleed for her as passionately
As I pen down verses.
For I am consumed by her being
And my blood paints her beauty
On this pierced canvas I call my heart.
The kindness fading within her eyes,
Fading as I hold her cheek,
She screams in disgust as this touch
She'd felt before. This touch, a memory
Of what once was, a promise once kept.
I smile again, feeling the warm blood
On the back of my tongue, elated
That she knew. This love abounding
Through the grave and beyond,
My soul it carries her, etched
Upon its crest, a symbol of reverence.
A love unforgotten, a vow kept.

Coffee

Atoms collide and the heavens die slow,
But my love for you remains steadfast,
Like the coffee that heals you on a chilly morning,
Pressed against your lips, waves of bitterness
And warmth collide to find the right balance
To soothe your kind soul. Mon Cherie, I pray
You find comfort in holding that cup of coffee
The way I rejuvenate my soul upon your
Autumn eyes and thine coffee-scented gaze.
I pray that cup of coffee brings you peace
As it touches the base of your cherry lip,
Like I seek solace upon your kind embrace.
I pray it warms your soul and pours life
Into you as you once did to me, tearing
Down my cold walls and breathing life into me.
Warming my once-dying heart to a rhyme
That whispers your name in every beat.
I pray you never grow weary of that cup
That tirelessly seeks to find favor in your eyes.
As atoms collide and the heavens die slow,
But I remain steadfast in my love for you, Mon Cherie.

Will You Remember Me Still?

Will you remember me still
when we meet years from now?

Will you remember me still?
Would you return to me
just as you were or would I
meet a stranger, a heart foreign
to the one I'd known?
Would you return to me
just as you were
or do I have to fall in love
with another you?

Will you remember me still?
Will you think of me fondly
the days passed with complete angst
of not being with one another?

Will you remember me still
as a lover or a villain?

Will you remember me still
as a book kept hidden on the shelf
or a candle that burnt down your walls?

Will you remember me still
as fondly as you did past autumn
or will you remember me still
as harshly as the scorching sun?

Underneath The Crescent Moon

The night sky glistened through the puddles
as he held her hand through the sidewalk.
The rain eased slowly to the ground,
as it felt neither bashful nor silent.
A wonderful symphony made eternal
upon their eyes that met one another
underneath the crescent moon.

Her hair drenched from the rain
laid plain upon her wondrous beauty,
as he gazed blinded with affection,
knowing he'd never experience again
such moments of elation for eons to come.
He treasured these moments,
as her eyes shined brighter than the arch
placed upon the dark canvas with lights
prickling through the threads woven together,
holding in place the grandeur of the universe,
all bland in comparison to those glistening eyes
underneath the Crescent moon.

Her hand laid comfortably within his palm,
as he led her further into the broken bridge.
The rain still pouring as he held on to her
more tightly than he'd held on before,
for he knew once they'd reach the edge,
the night would end and her hand would fade,
yet he still walked forth hoping she might stay,
desperate for a miracle praying for the rain
to consume him whole to lay with her
before the sounds of judgement
awaken him from this ecstasy,
rid him of the one he craved the most
underneath the crescent moon.

Awaken he did to the cursed bells,
light thrust upon his scarred brow,
as a blade piercing through bare skin,
this torment unending, he cries in pain,
chiding the day for it ripped apart his soul.
He craved to sleep again to rest without care,
to wish for her deeply his heart could not bear,
as the blade painted red this mortal corpse,
a wish granted a miracle fulfilled
upon the broken bridge he rests,
her hand upon his pierced chest he smiles,
"Here I find you again", said he,
basked under the glory of the night,

as his heart grew faint and his breath lay still,
where upon his eyes met hers
underneath the crescent moon.

The Lakeview

Where upon the lakeview
thine eyes met mine,
visions of rapture come true,
everlasting divine, wondrous beauty.
Will thou stay here beside mine,
render care and comfort
for my wearied soul?
My heart doth leap for joy,
this overwhelms mine senses,
enchanting reservoirs of love
bursting forth in deep trenches.

As the sun bids farewell
and the waters quiet down,
I knew not this moment would cease,
as your beauty fades from my side.
Mine ears no longer remember
the sound of your voice,
nor mine nose the smell upon
thine brow. Mine hands remember
no more the skin they once held close.
If I am no more, a coffin
nailed with grief unending,

my existence seems futile, for I am
but a rotting carcass burdened
with pain of memories past.

This haunting memory doth torture
my soul, it neither grieves nor repulses.
These memories seemingly transient,
a facade mine mind put forth.
This lakeview exists and I do too,
yet you, Mon Cherie, are but a dream,
the final chapter from a book unread,
burnt to ashes its pages I still keep.

They were but visions
cast upon mine being.
This tormented soul knows not
what farewells mean in this hell.
He seeketh to hold close
moments of care and comfort,
unknowing of the pain he brings upon,
suffocating the one he treasures most,
naive entity, return to carnage,
for thy compassion means death
in this hellish incarnate.

But your name I carry with me,
etched upon mine epitaph.
I lay patiently in waiting,
sat alone near waters mild,
whence we shall find each other,
and mine heart rejoice, bursting
forth in gladness, everlasting
spring of comfort and care,
where upon the lakeview
thine eyes met mine.

Waxen Candle

When the waxen candle dies slow,
As I gaze into a waning flame,
I look up to her glistening eyes,
Reveal a wonder I thought fiction.
This dying flame illuminating
Such grace I knew not existed,
Of this world nor any other.
Her cherry wine lips glittered
as she smiled still glancing below,
that dying flame forevermore,
as time stood frozen and mine
eyes still unwavering, her beauty
unblemished, this moment I'd paint
to immortalize her image, a painting
worth more than ruby or gold.

The flame begins to flicker
As her eyes meet mine own.
I come across not wonder
But a numbing sadness beneath.
Her glowing eyes now dim.
She gazes fondly at me, her face
Easing to the side as she forces
A smile, one unlike the former.

This smile, a keepsake of things untold,
Of regrets kept hidden, of the guilt
Swallowed whole, a smile worth
A novel written in sand, memorized
In the ocean, barely afloat.
A smile that wrecked mine soul,
A sunken ship with fortunes abandon.

As the dying flame comes to a still,
And the motions of time resume,
With one final gaze into her eyes,
I smile, one filled with acceptance
Of things unforgotten, of memories
Lived together and moments etched
In mine heart, a smile worth a painting,
A novel, and a fortune unsold.
I remain smiling as the light dims slow,
And the shadows seep into nothingness.
Her glistening eyes no more,
As her face disappears into the night.
I remain frozen watching a sight,
Unable to hold on to a flame.
She vanishes into the darkness,
And so do I…

The Bus Ride

As the horn sirened ahead,
the crowd rushing forth,
as I feel your shoulder graze mine,
the bus moving slow, speak softly
into mine ears, the crowd unaware
of that soft graze upon my shoulder.
Mine eyes gazing into yours
as you whisper words infinite.
My heart grows fonder each hour
to be here with you, gazing
out the window, the streets,
the roar of engines, sirens,
noises that seep into silence,
as we gaze into each other,
knowing how painful it will be,
grief purchased from a future
with present minutes' worth gold.
My shoulder will never feel your touch,
nor mine ears hear the whispers
infinite in this moment but it fades,
as all things do, this moment it fades.
As the bus comes to a halt, motionless,
I watch her leave, carrying her bags,
a smile upon her lips she looks back,
just as she steps to the ground.

The excitement of the journey,
sat together amidst the crowd,
the smile now fades into a final whisper.
I fear this is the end, I hear no more
whispers from her lips that sang a melody,
now read words of an epitaph,
a memory worth carrying,
now set in a coffin afraid to open.
The bus now set in motion,
and I am alone gazing through
the window as I feel a pain,
a tug runs through my chest,
a red light, the bus nears a halt,
and I close mine eyes.
I feel her touch upon my shoulder,
her whispers still echoing in my ear.

Beating Heart

I carry with me the stones that mark a grave,
etched on these stones, a sad lullaby,
a cautionary tale sung for the lovers without,
songs written on these stones, a wise oath,
to rid thineself of love's wretched sword,
to tear thine own heart and place it anew
in her hands now rest a beating virtue,
to crush or care for, I rest with her will,
lest I die, I shall awe in wonder still,
a dilemma causeth mine mind to wander,
mine heart lay still before I ever saw her,
now it lays still once more,
since after she claimed it of virtue no more,

and yet for a brief moment,
in her warm hands, my heart findeth its strength,
to beat a beat, it remembered long ago,
in those moments of warmth and nurture,
this heart of mine found its true nature.
Now it lays silent inside that grave,
waiting for tomorrow come,
whence it hopes to find itself
in the once warm hands that held it close,
to beat a beat that sounds familiar,

to be cared for and nurtured still,
this heart of mine I can't help but wonder,
this blinded hope so eager to surrender.

Pride is the Devil

Cradled in her warmth, I find myself bare,
cushioned by her grace, I seek no despair,
her precious hands intertwined in mine,
fair maiden's love richer than fine wine.
Wars I'd wage to seek favor in her eyes,
no mortal could orchestrate my demise,
my blade shall run true and more swift,
to bear witness for my love and uplift
my weakened body to righteous ecstasy,
sober upheaval, an end to mine fantasy.
Mine pride shall rue the day it soar
up above yonder hills and far more,
rest assured her fall doth come soon,
no bird shall fly when comes its doom,
broken wings, I find myself bare again,
yet maiden's warmth I could not attain,
I yearn for her touch, her caring embrace,
but all that I seek I could never replace.
I soon come to realize mine fatal flaw
mine pride in mine love obsessive and raw
caused greater conflict in her to resist
carnal wretchedness in mine that persist.
Fare ye well my fair maiden's kiss
Thou shalt endure in my heart's bliss.
I learneth now this fall from grace

Mine pride it slithered in broken face,
a woeful façade, a merry smile it lept,
took long abode in mine heart it kept.
Woe to me, I weep, this broken soul
No maiden shall touch this burning coal.
Be her doth fair or wretched still,
yet mine ambition shall cause her ill.
I pray, I weep, I seek a cure to mend
This pride of mine shall rue its end.
For whence the day shall come on hand
My blade shall pierce it true and stand,
wretched serpent, thou shalt perish still
and watch mine rise to grace uphill.
Whence I shalt my fair maiden find,
this time her hand and mine intertwined,
for no more shall that serpent defy,
fair maiden's kiss shall no longer deny.
Those fangs of evil shall I endure,
a heart of humility shall I procure,
for with meekness comes virtue fulfilled,
mine heart shall it heal and more so rebuild.

Grail

If there was ever a moment in time
Where mine eyes hadn't gazed upon
Your beauty, I would slit my wrists
To offer a sacrifice of guilt confessing
My arduous iniquity, blatant transgression.
This cup filled to the brim I cannot withhold,
Passions run deeper than Kubla's grove,
I bleed upon the thorns of my conviction,
A commandment not forsaken.
My love for you shall remain unblemished,
I lay down my life for thine pleasure,
I lay down my life for kind measure.
I bear no musings of lust nor ill will,
Mine intentions neither wander nor stray,
Mine intentions speak truth and not decay.
Come swiftly and hold my cup well,
For it brims with crimson red, it swell,
Harness mine love and treat it well,
For it shall endure the darkest nights,
Mon Cherie, speak mine kind name,
Shall I appear before thine in vengeful rain,
No storm, no earth, no fire shall keep
This heart doth seeks to find thy smile,
Behest mine heart and shall it trail,
For thine love to win my life's true grail.

Soul

Fallen Crown

Worthy of a throne, this man of valor,
Strength in his bones armed with grace.
Judgment befitting Solomon, arise,
For he doth a king of righteous work.

Blinded veil removed, a question abound,
Hamartian law in him it findeth flaw.
His pride and wrath doth rue his creed,
Fear shall conjure its poison beneath.

Shall it overtake him in somber roots,
Deep within spaces he knew not existed?
Shall it devour him whole to a dry bone,
A king on his throne, a dead carcass it rots?

The Son shall find His father in shackles,
Untrained in battle and brittle in sight.
Yet shall He wage war for His father's sin,
Come victorious, no pride within Him.

Unbound by fear and mortal decay,
The son doth set his shackles free.
Shall He crown him king once more,
His sword shall he hold and roar.

This king shall he return to be,
Unburdened by sin and rite agony.
Glory restored shall Glory remain,
For The Son shall his father attain.

A Shattered Glass

Restless and hurting, a cause for worry,
This thirst for excitement I wish could bury.
Such rage and impatience, a ghastful reflection,
A glass of whiskey seems to draw one's attention.

A burning sensation, a flavorful scent,
Masking worry and anxious thought well sent.
Inebriated self, a being of free will,
An unconscious self he could finally be still.

The surrender to temptation,
A hollow sense of self, a bland imitation.
He would soon find to regret
A failing escape to a long drawn debt,
A debt to oneself, a debt of accountability,
To live a life of peace and mental stability.

He finds himself a cutting blade,
Moments of hesitation, his emotions fade.
Numb throughout, a trembling fist,
Inches close to severing one's wrist.
Moments away from eternal damnation,
He thought it better than living in desperation.

Armageddon

Red wine and sweet melons,
A day of bliss and joy for the dark felons.
Banquet of thieves and a garland of thorns,
To crown these beings cunning murderous fawns.

A devilish feast for the dark disciples,
A familiar sight of polished grey fables.
Sitting high on their castles of woe,
Soon to be forgotten, banished in fiery snow.

Rejoicing unknowing the plague that would befall,
Reckless in carnage, soon to meet the fate of Saul.
Blinded by greed and lust for meat,
Fueled by devils they dare not defeat.

Bouquet of bones and plates of food,
The carnal desire to kill, a fearful dark mood.
Bottles of whiskey and cases of gin,
Aromas of unfiltered rage and melancholy within.

Raging oceans and vengeful tides,
Blaring alarms, the earth it rises.
Mother nature seeketh her rapture,
A bloody end for this tyrannic venture.

Red wine and sweet melons,
Walls painted red, the death of the dark felons.
An Armageddon meal worth dying for?
An Armageddon meal worth killing for?

Book

Closing a chapter is hard,
But burning the book in entirety
Chips away parts of one's soul.
Watching each page burn fiercely,
So fiercely, so bright, overwhelmingly bright.
Unable to embrace such glorious grief,
Does one become numb, staring into a mirror
With a rusted blade tearing through
The remnants of what once was,
Unable to feel what once could be felt.

Veins

Hold a blade to these veins,
Watch it pen down verses of haunting romance.
Verses of a candlelight too pure for a sinner,
Verses of a lighthouse during a rainstorm.
Verses of fairy light in the darkest of days
And verses of perfume that smell like home.
The red will wash away his sins,
And the flame will scar his tissue.
But he will forever cherish these scars,
For they penned down verses-
He could never erase from these walls.

Confession

I await the days I can find light in the darkness.
I await the days the light finds me.
I yearn for the days when I stop praying for forgiveness.
I yearn for the days when I am forgiven.
I pray for the days when the nights don't haunt me.
I pray for the days my dreams come true.
I ache for the days I find solitude in my being.
I ache for the days I can adore myself.
I wish for the days I can feel without pain.
I wish for the days I can care for someone again.
I long for the days I can love everything around me.
I long for the days everything around loves me.
My desire to be whole again,
To face life earnestly without pain again,
To learn to love and lose without drain again,
To foster care and miss someone without ache again,
To jump around and dance in the rain again,
To forget bad memories and pray again,
To live life without guilt again,
To live life without guilt again.

Pheonix

Find him calm and sullen,
Under the bridges of dessert streams.
A tree house to sheath him,
From the glowing furnace of these pages.
Sandcastles built on the harsh seas,
And poetry written on loose soil, washed away,
Left forgotten. Scarred tissue and burnt skin,
Suffocating breath and crushed within.
A soul striving, struggling, panting.
A spirit squeezing its last breath,
A watch ticking till its last step,
The sound of the nail piercing through the coffin.
Oh, but wait! This fire could never consume him,
Nor the waves swallow his soul.
A heart rebuilt on ash and fairy dust.
A soul rebuilt in the depths of the cosmos
Amongst the angels in heaven.
Those burning embers will paint his story,
The thrashing waves will tell his tale.
The tale of a man, the tale of a man,
Who became so much more.

Love & Lies

Gloomy days and sinister nights,
I pray the fair maiden you are but alone.
This hellish world illusioned with glittery lights,
A trusted companion will serve as a sacral rune.
Wear thine heart on thy sleave,
But let not false prophets to reach you as they please.
Keep your mind filled with love and always believe,
Better days will appear and thine heart bleeding shall cease.

Dark and corrupt a man's soul. this present day,
Filled with intention of lust and pain.
Let not this would horrid reality keep you at bay,
Let out your wings, the wide world is yours to gain.
Diamonds and gold are but a fool's joy,
Set thine hearts on lasting love and loyalty.
A patient soul not a heart of troy,
Live each day for you are royalty.

Unspoken

The wind blows, I pick myself up,
Held my bag tight, my umbrella tighter.
Cover myself with a large coat,
Walking along the narrow street.

Noises behind the dark alley:
A little child throwing stones,
A little pup yelping in pain.
I walk along the narrow street.

The mother screams and heaves,
The boy kicks her to the side,
The mother yelping in pain.
I walk along the narrow street.

The boy laughs hysterically,
His friends cheer him on.
The boy throwing stones,
I walk along the narrow street.

The stone now skipped my way,
Hit my knee and wobbled away.
I find myself yelping in pain.
I walk along the narrow street.

The mother, the pup, and I —
Cries of pain and misery abide.
The man's laughter echoes.
I crawl along the narrow street.

A Murder

The wintery veil of sadness withers
As light pierces through the canopy.
The morning sun shone bright
As the dove's melody echoes in the sky.
Hope granted and joy renewed,
The boy sits by his window,
Keen to bask in the summer breath
And mellow in the yellow shone.

Voices elated, and as the boy peers across
The window to find huddles of men,
Grasping at children and hugging them tight,
Shouts of joy and gladness abound.
The boy delights in his sight throughout—
The sight of men crying and women silent,
The sight of intimate love and vulnerable silence,
The sight, it blinds as the yellow shone bright.

The boy looks farther into the yellow sun,
The wind grew deeper, and fearfully it ran.
His brow now filled with pools of sweat,
And the heat makes his face blush red.
Unable to bear the heat, he runs;

To hide beneath the shade, he runs.
"Mother, mother!" he shouts and screams,
"Mother, mother!" He sees yellow and screams.

Silence now, the yellow has vanished.
The dove's melody heard no more,
The morning sun, it sets in silence,
Afraid to see this mortal violence.
Hope ripped away and joy unfound,
The boy sits by his window,
His ashes now mixed with glass;
The boy sits still and violence laughs.

The mother rushes forth, silent in rite,
As her feet bleed from the rubble.
She walks valiantly with all her might,
The shards of glass now pierce her palm.
As she carries her child in her bleeding arm,
Silent still, she carries him forth.
"Son, son, I'm here now, my love."
"Son, son?" For 'twas a murder, not a dove.

Rage

Listen to the echoes of the drums,
bursting forth to claim their victory.
They shy not away from bloodshed,
nor do they clamor for treaties.
Vengeance called upon their lands,
and they answered with fiery souls.
They heed not to reason nor rest,
minds so corrupted with wrath.
Rage ensues like a gushing river,
blazing past the mountains,
paving its way through untrodden
lands and ripping apart the soil
held together since ages past.
Their hearts hardened with the cries
of their younglings and widows,
their hearts bleeding from the cries
of their mothers and dead fathers.
They rage, rage against the gods,
the ones they once worshipped,
the ones they believed their savior.
They rage, not as mortals with frailty
in their bones, not as cowards with fear,
but as kings, kings of glory and wrath,
kings of bravery and grit they rage.
What once was lost shall no longer

be regained, their hearts now vanish,
and what remains be made of stone.
Warriors, was thine vengeance fulfilled?
Have thy drank thine fill of wrath and more?
Is thine cup that once ranneth over, empty?
Have you found your peace or rather
do you still lay awake?
For vengeance, dear brethren,
it was never yours to take.

Chosen

Reaching Out

Masked faces, trembling in the dark,
Afraid to seek out the light,
Writhing in agony, fearful of the sun,
This guilt too heavy a burden to bear,
Drowning further in a fiery lake,
Gasping for precious air.
Afraid to reach out to the heavens,
Where does my help come from?
It comes from you, Lord,
Still by my hurting side,
Unafraid to reach out,
Abounding in love, a wounded palm,
To hold secure my broken heart.
This burden eased, my shoulders free,
I lift my eyes to the mountains,
For once more I am free.

Greater Purpose

Greater purpose I crave,
This mortal casket I despise.
I am burdened by my pleasures,
A rotten core masked with scented roses.
But my petals wither as I am left
Barren in the cold unfriendly desert.
I fear I am too far from salvation,
As I lay trampled on the coarse sand.
Far be it for a deeper longing,
I am too afraid to hope,
For a sip from a cup,
Even to drink my own blood.
I am too afraid this poison
Would neither kill nor let live.
It doth rot more and slow,
Slower than I seek abandon,
Slower than I desire the numb.
A sip I beg anything untouched
By these rotten hands of mine.
I am afraid It will turn to ash,
But my hands move desperate,
In search of something pure.
Something unblemished I wail,
"Stop this madness, you are beyond repair."
"All you touch becomes a rotting soul."

"Stop," I cry to myself, but these hands,
They touch your garment,
These hands, they hold your cup,
These hands, they let me drink your blood.
Tears blinding my senses as I glimpse
At my own hands. Yours intertwined in mine,
They held me calm, wiped my tears,
Quenched my thirst, made me whole.
A rose as red as once shed on the cross,
A heart made anew as you gave me yours.
Greater purpose I no longer crave,
For I am reborn from a rotting grave.

Conviction

Peace like no other, a calm in the sea.
Rest well, my son, a battle hard fought.
Remember your stead, a loyal guardian,
keeping you safe within your soul.
Keep away from guilt, a fool's lie.
Rest easy in conviction, a man's pride.
Lie waiting patiently for a second upheaval.
Keep thine armor ready, wear it daily.
Let thine blade shine bright, shield kept near.
Forget not your King, His riches beyond compare.
His love greater than the ocean, His heart infinite,
He shelters the weak, He arms the broken.
He purifies your silver, let your faith be unshaken.
Steadfast in your prayer, keep faith in waiting,
as the end draws near, my son, lay patient.
Your reward much greater than mortal desire,
the kingdom await, its faithful servant.
Rejoice and be glad, a judgement broken.

Battle Won

Come barren as ye lay to the altar,
Be thou washed by His blood made whole.
Righteous sinner 'tis thou art folly,
Thine pride shall rue the day you bore.
This mortal battle thou canst wage alone,
Thine threshold for pain and suffering low.
Seek first His throne and be thou filled,
For He hath won the battle still.

Thou must and must alone seek Him,
For in thy battle thine spirit weaken.
His grace shall comfort and care offer,
A feast in full measure accept,
For thy battle scars mean nothing less
Than dust and sand laid across the sea.
For His feast doth have no fee but
To acknowledge Him king and all for thee.

'Tis all you need to sing His praise,
His courts, His throne, immortal embrace.
Seek first His throne and be thou filled,
All ye know and knoweth still
Shall fade and rot and be gone tomorrow.

Yet His grace, His love shall never depart,
Coming of times this desperate hour,
Let ye not lose hope or scatter sour.

Deny thine flesh this battle pursue,
Thou might be broken and yet rejoice,
For His coming is near, shall ye rejoice,
Siren the trumpets and kneel O mortal,
Surrender yet now thine wearied soul.
Here cometh the Christ,
Shall ye acknowledge Him whole.

Fruition

Relentless pursuit, His hands nailed to the cross,
love unconditional, I find myself unworthy,
guilty of sin and shame abounding,
yet His grace that saveth me today,
a wish upon a wishing well ran dry,
a prayer to the bottle, a genie unmade,
I find myself upon a tree hanging low,
mine fruit that rotten in disgust,
this fruit no earth, no moth, no slime would digest,
a fruit so rotten it lays decay all around,
and yet His hands, His pierced hands,
still picked it up.
He washed it whole in His own blood
and planted anew in fertile ground.
A seed, a rain, a blossoming leaf,
I find myself a new morn to see.
This fruit I bear is not mine own,
but sheds a taste of glory untold.
His grace, His love, so pure, so true,
I find myself in the spring of youth.
Mine fruit, they find it comforteth them.
I tell 'tis not mine but my Father's stem.
His vine art true, and I His branch,
to bear fruit, mine duty through His blood,
till yonder day comes raining forth,

and I shall sit by His side betrothed,
in mine the bride, in His the groom,
a love everlasting, forever it bloom,
and all shall know and worship Him,
the one whose hands were nailed with sin,
and crown Him King, alleluia,
forever and always, alleluia.

www.ingramcontent.com/pod-product-compliance
Lightning Source LLC
LaVergne TN
LVHW041109150826
845673LV00007B/1980

* 9 7 9 8 8 9 5 5 6 5 5 8 2 *

Introduction
Hearing them speak

Part I

This project began in my lunch break, one day in November 2005. I had been co-ordinating a subject at university, entitled Literary Classics and one of the key texts for study was Harold Bloom's *The Western Canon: The Books and School of the Ages*. After a discussion in one of the tutorials about Shakespeare's place in the canon, I said, 'I agree with Harold Bloom on this one.' A student said, 'You love Harold Bloom', and the rest is history, as they say. In the final week of classes, I doctored a photo so that Bloom and I were standing side by side in a heart-shaped frame. It got a round of applause. I was 'outed' as a Bloomite and the students had, what many of them identified as, the best and most memorable semester in Literary Studies. I'd forged an imaginary relationship with Bloom, built solely on my reading of his oeuvre, the media surrounding him and my teaching of his Western Canon to third year undergraduates.

When I discovered I was heading to Boston and New York with a group of students on a study tour in January, 2006, I thought of Bloom. I sat down at my desk, opened my laptop and trawled the web until I found his email address at Yale. I thought that there was very little chance he would answer my email but I knew that he had known my supervisor, Chris Wallace-Crabbe, when Chris had been a Harkness Fellow at Yale, so I decided to use that relationship to hopefully convince him that I wasn't a crazed e-stalker.

Less than twelve hours later, I received the following response:

> Dear Cassandra:
> I am likely to be home in January. My phone in New Haven is 203 XXX XXXX. Otherwise, try my phone in NYC 212 XXX XXXX. Kind regards to Chris.
> Harold Bloom

Whatever I had said in that email, or perhaps my contact with Chris, had convinced him to send his private phone numbers in an email. I still have them in my phone, even though I only had to ring the New Haven number once. I just like them being there and I like the thought that my list of contacts includes one of my favourite scholars. This is how this book of interviews was born. Although, in 2005, all I envisaged was a chance to meet and interview Bloom and publish the interview in a literary journal. It snowballed from there. If Bloom had responded, I considered that more of my idols might respond, too.

At the top of my interview wish list was Camille Paglia. My copy of *Sexual Personae*, Paglia's groundbreaking book of criticism, is well thumbed and I still set her chapter on Emily Dickinson as compulsory reading in poetry classes. I have always been impressed by Paglia; in a literary world full of sycophants, she doesn't toe the line.

Paglia wasn't as easy to contact as Bloom. It is understandable, given her prominence in the media. I wrote her a letter and sent it, snail mail, to the University of the Arts in Philadelphia. She emailed me back via a personal routing service and I developed a 'relationship' with the person who delivered her emails. She agreed to meet me at a bar and restaurant in Wilmington, Virginia. I remember thinking how apt it was that I had to walk through the Tubman-Garret Riverfront Park to get to the restaurant. The courage of individuals is a theme that Wilmington embraces and Paglia, in her own way, is revolutionary.

So the project began quite selfishly. I made a list of people I admired and started approaching them for an interview. Initially, that was Jim Cullen, James Green, Paul Kane, Todd Gitlin, Howard Zinn and even the former Chairman of the National Endowment for the Arts, Dana Gioia. They were scholars whose work I introduced to my students; they were writers whose work I devoured.

While I initially thought these scholars, intellectuals and writers had no connection, other than as being on my own personal wish list, I started to see a web of connections forming. Bloom was Paglia's supervisor and Greenblatt's teacher. In their interviews these scholars commented on each other. Gioia discussed Paglia's work, and she, in turn discussed his essays on poetry. Cullen discussed Jackson's views on history in education, which I then followed up in his interview. Finding the links was particularly exciting and rewarding. But I do not pretend that this is a balanced or objective selection of scholars, writers and intellectuals. It is simply, *my* selection, based on *my* reading and *my* opportunities coupled with *my* experience in the world.

It is important to acknowledge that I developed this project as I went along and so my purpose shifted a number of times, across the years. Initially, I was hoping just to publish one interview. After my interview with Bloom was published in the University of California's *Writing on the Edge,* the editors, Eric Schroeder and John Boe, expressed interest in publishing more of my interviews. So I extended my plan and decided to publish what I thought would be 'a few more' interviews. In this way, I had an initial audience: the readership of the journal. It was a symbiotic relationship, my interests overlapped with the interests of the journal: writing and the teaching of writing became my focus.

But I also interviewed people who didn't totally fit the journal's brief. I wanted to stay true to my intention of interviewing people I found interesting, so, publishing in a journal was always secondary to this more personal commitment. I sought out journals such as *Australasian Journal of American Studies* post-interview, rather than having specific journals in mind during the interview. It would be misleading to imply that I didn't make the most of the opportunities that were presented to me. Some scholars were available at the times I was travelling to the United States, but I remained steadfast in my choice to interview those scholars, intellectuals and writers I felt had somehow got 'under my skin'.

Therefore, it is fair to say that with every interview I would redefine the scope of my investigation. By placing the interviews in chronological order, I hope the reader will be able to see these progressions in both my interviews and the overarching investigation take place. While I began with an interest in reading, teaching and the academy, the project began to morph into a study of the public intellectual in the ivory tower. This necessitated incorporating more questions on the role and responsibility of these individuals – something that interested me most about public intellectuals.

More recently, my purpose has shifted again. By collecting these interviews in a book, my intention is to inform and entertain a wide readership. It doesn't matter whether or not the reader is familiar with any of the writers, scholars and intellectuals; what they have to say is interesting. Teaching, reading, politics, history and writing are universally engaging topics and the interviewees' comments are often striking and perceptive. Each interview is an enjoyable reading experience, but readers also have the option of dipping into any or all of them.

These interviews can stand alone, but as a collection of essays they work in juxtaposition to comment a variety of themes. Comparing Chomsky's response to the questions concerning the role and responsibility of public intellectual with Zinn's, Kane's, Gitlin's and Green's unearths some pithy differences and similarities. All of them mention honesty, in some capacity, as essential; Chomsky is the only one to divide the category into dissident and subservient public intellectuals. Similarly, comparing Paglia's views on poetry with Harold Bloom's, Paul Kane's and Dana Gioia's is a worthwhile exercise, as together they present a united front on the importance of reading poetry.

In each interview, I was hoping to make discoveries about each writer, intellectual and scholar that could not be found on the internet, nor in any book, nor journal. For instance, I wanted to ask Jim Cullen why he had such an affinity with people in history, like Springsteen, Reagan and Lincoln. And then more personally, I wanted to know if he had ever tried writing fiction and how he found time to write so many books and teach full time. Similarly, I wanted to ask Howard Zinn about his life as an academic at Boston University and his teaching style. In the end, I discovered far more than the answers to my questions. The incredibly generous spirit of the interviewees meant that I became part of their day and was given an insight into their respective worlds. The conversation before and after the interview allowed me into the more casual and intimate moments and I was also able to see how others responded to the interviewee: secretaries, personal assistants, partners and lovers. And, of course, the meeting places were also an insight into the spaces they inhabited and felt most at home. This varied from Greenblatt's and Chomsky's offices to Bloom's, Gitlin's and Zinn's homes and even University House at the University of Melbourne where I interviewed Paul Kane on one of his annual trips to Australia.

I have always been committed to the role of unobtrusive interviewer. I have a policy not to interrupt the interviewee; nor to share my own anecdotes, unless I am pressed; just to concentrate on being a facilitator. For this reason, using the Q and A style for my publications is important. When the interviewer composes an article based on an interview and prioritises what to quote and what to leave out, there is a different sense of authenticity and authorship. In this way, when the interviewer makes conclusions about how the interviewee is feeling or reacting to the interview, then it becomes more about the interviewer than the subject's voice. The interviews in this collection prioritise the writers', intellectuals' and scholars' voices. As the answers are published verbatim, the reader is encouraged to draw his/her own interpretations from the words spoken. Where interviews ran longer than the publication space available, entire questions were edited out, rather than summarising or removing parts of the response.

A short introduction to each interview acts as a framing device informing the reader why the person was interviewed and where the interview took place. I hope that readers will, to some extent, be able to visualise the bar in which I met Camille Paglia, or the JFK museum where I interviewed James Green or the classroom at Columbia University with Kenneth T. Jackson sitting in a chair on a raised platform.

Part II

The most important feature of the interviews in this book is, for the most part, that they do not repeat information that can be found elsewhere, especially on the internet. Many interviewees commented favourably on the questions they were asked because of this decision to avoid repetition. People are inevitably disappointed when they are asked the same questions and when faced with this situation often give a stock standard response. This is a waste of time for everyone and exposes an interviewer who has not done his/her research. Furthermore, this does not build a positive relationship between the interviewer and interviewee.

In these interviews, each question was formulated, not only to be open ended and thus allow for a longer and more detailed response, but also to try and elicit something more personal. For this reason, I embrace people straying from the topic. Why contain these writers, intellectuals and scholars to the bounds of the questions? They are deeply interesting people. It has always made for fascinating tangents, stories and rhythms in the interview to let them move freely from one idea to the next. In these instances it is important to consider where the person is directing the interview and why he/she is doing this. If the original question is important, it is easy to go back and ask the same question if he or she hasn't really answered it.

Most importantly, I have learned the art of not filling gaps and silences. While it is often tempting to alleviate the tension that a silence can create in an interview, it is often after one of these silences that something really interesting will be offered. To jump in with the next question, or deflect attention away from the silence can be more detrimental than positive.

The interviews in this collection were all undertaken in person. Although it would have been possible to interview a greater range of people if I had been prepared to conduct interviews over the telephone, this was not my purpose. I wanted to meet people. This is key to any good interview as it allows the interviewer to adjust questions, improvise and extend discussions based on readings of body language and other observations. But mostly, it makes a better impression to interview someone in person and this results in a better experience for all. I think interviews by Skype or phone are impaired because there is an unbreachable distance and you can often feel this in the transcript.

There were some failed attempts to connect with people. A number of people either didn't respond or informed me they were too busy to be interviewed at the time I was travelling to the United States. There were many other writers, intellectuals and scholars I would have liked to meet and interview, but I was limited to the dates and location of my travels and work commitments. This explains why all of the interviews in this collection are with people residing or working on the east coast of America; this is where I conduct my business. It also explains, in part, the abundance of white, male middleclass writers, intellectuals and scholars. There would have been more women and a representative sample of other minority groups if all of the people I approached had been available or had agreed to be interviewed.

Finally, my Australian origin is an important part of my interviews. For American journals, Australian references and questions were often edited out. I have put them back, here, for the Australian reader. People I contacted were interested in Australia and, more specifically, Australian literature, politics and history. In many cases, I believe it is this Australian connection that was decisive in securing so many interviews.

Part III

Professor Leon Cantrell has identified my investigations into American public intellectuals in academe as 'a striking example of research inventiveness and innovation.' He adds, 'Building on the earlier model of the *Paris Review* interviews with major writers, she has applied a similar methodology to a group of contemporary intellectuals whose role and significance is then analysed not just in terms of what they write, but also in terms of what they say and of how they respond to incisive and well-researched questioning.'

The *Paris Review* has been instrumental in my development as an interviewer; since my teenage years I have voraciously read their 'Writers at Work' interviews. My favourite interviews are with Vladimir Nabokov, Dorothy Parker, Francoise Sagan and Woody Allen. I have also been influenced by Charlie Rose's interviews and even the fun and improvisational nature of *Inside the Actors Studio* hosted by James Lipton. The interviews in this book are also a timely response to Dana Gioia's, Russell Jacoby's and Richard Posner's debate on the pros and cons of public intellectuals working in academe. With further study in mind, a series of questions specific to the role and responsibility of the public intellectual were posed, in addition to individual questions based on the interviewee's publications and expertise. In this way, answers can and should be compared and contrasted.

In transcribing these interviews I have tried to retain the cadence of each interviewee's speech. I like to uses dashes to stand in for changes in thought mid-sentence, rather than re-writing a sentence so that it becomes syntactically correct. Sentences that trail off or morph into something else, as well as idiosyncrasies in speech, all serve to highlight the individuality of each writer, intellectual and scholar. It is in these moments that you can 'hear' them speak.

'Deep Subjectivity' *Harold Bloom*

Most kids have posters of rock stars or actors on their bedroom walls; I had pictures of Harold Bloom. After reading The Anxiety of Influence: A Theory of Poetry, *I devoured everything he wrote.* The Western Canon *is my favourite book and I subject my students in Literary Classics at The University of Melbourne to many chapters of his work and wit. He says he comes out of the Northrup Frye tradition and I tell everyone that I come out of the Bloom tradition. I bloomed with Bloom. His publication record is formidable; his internal library is one akin to the Royal Library of Alexandria. He can quote from millions of different sources and makes incredible web-like connections between them, substantiating his view with more quotations from the primary texts. His emphasis on the texts, themselves, and his defence of 19th century Romantic poetry is what I find most appealing. And of course, who can resist his controversial comments about Feminist, Marxist, New Historicist and Post Modernist critiques of literature and other forms of academic criticism, which are daring—often titillating? If Bloom is denounced as elitist, then I find myself allying myself to him; there is a hierarchy in literature and I'm interested in reading the best: I only have one lifetime. His life's work has culminated in two incredibly elevated positions in academia. Bloom is currently a Sterling Professor of the Humanities at Yale University and was Berg Professor of English and American Literature at New York University until 2004.*

I fly to Boston on business and buy a train ticket to New Haven. When I get to New Haven I hail a taxi which takes me to his house (he also has an apartment in New York). It is cold but I am hot, sweaty and nervous in my pink parka. My backpack is full of all the books I want him to sign and it weighs me down. Bloom lives in a gingerbread house and as I walk up to the door, classical music wafts out through the doorjamb. After he greets me and takes my jacket, Bloom tells me that he is having surgery in the next few days. He looks quite well but I can see that he is a little stressed and preoccupied, that is, until I begin asking my questions and he becomes animated and charismatic. His wife is in the lounge room, reading. I suspect she's there to ascertain whether or not I am an antagonistic postmodernist. She leaves when she realises I'm not and he takes me in to sit at the kitchen table. He gives me a copy of Where Wisdom is Found *and politely signs my bag full of his books. Then I sit, perched on the edge of my seat and begin asking my questions.*

CA I never get tired of hearing how much you love teaching, your passion for teaching.

BLOOM I still do. I have a new semester starting at Yale next week. At Yale, if you're a full professor, you teach five semesters in a row and then you get a semester off to do your own work. I was out for a year with an open-heart operation and a bad reaction to it. But since then I've taught five semesters, two and a half years, so I have this term off. I'll turn seventy-six next July, but I will come back next September and begin another cycle of five terms on and one term off. Then I'll have to make a decision about the cycle after that because I will have turned seventy-nine and I don't think there is any precedent for anybody quite that old continuing to teach at Yale. Perhaps there is but I don't know.

I don't think I used to be a very good teacher because I talked too much. But now in old age I don't have the driving energy that I used to and I've found that sheer lack of overdrive had begun to help me as a teacher. I was much more patient in asking questions and not just answering them myself.

CA You've said you also find that you bring a lot of yourself to your teaching and that you can be very personal when you're teaching …

BLOOM I am, unfortunately, an extremely personal writer, as you know. And I've been denounced as an instance of what is called the 'personalist heresy', but I really don't know what they are talking about because as I have frequently said in print and out of it, objectivity, in what calls itself literary criticism, is always shallow and superficial. Subjectivity takes you a lifetime to authentically establish, and only, I think, what arises out of a deep subjectivity can ultimately be of use to anyone.

CA I think students find that really appealing—if you are willing to give a bit of yourself and talk about your own experiences they are more trusting …

BLOOM I'm afraid in my case I give rather too much of myself but it is a definite part of who I am.

(Harold's wife, Jean, comes home at this point.)
(to Jean): Oh you're holding up pretty well.
(to CA): I was worried about her because she went off to see the doctor.
(to Jean): You're back. Did you take that pill?
(to CA): I'm a terrible worrywart. Also, you see me a little more jumpy than usual because my heart has a flutter now and it beats too slowly, so they are going to take me in overnight next Wednesday and give me a pacemaker—though I'm assured, as a friend in New York who is a doctor said, 'Think of it as a tune-up, not even as a procedure, let alone an operation.'

CA When can you come home from that?

BLOOM Well I hope, if no complications develop, I will be away from my wife for only one night, Wednesday, and they'll let me home on Thursday. I think that is standard now with a pacemaker.

CA That's OK, I'd be a little jumpy, too! I want to ask you why you think the teaching profession is so often maligned. In Australia teachers aren't always well respected.

BLOOM Australia is a very strange country for one thing. I know this only from a distance as I have never been in Australia and … at my advanced age I rather doubt that Jean and I will ever get on an aeroplane again, let alone go back to Europe, let alone go off to the ends of the earth.

I do know a lot of Australian novelists. There is Elliot Perlman, whom my wife and I know and met in New York, together with his young lady, Deborah. Also, Peter Carey, John Kinsella, Thomas Keneally, who are very nice. I did not know, of course, the best of the Australian novelists, Patrick White. I still think *Riders in the Chariot* is the best novel to come out of Australia. I get the impression from talking to Kevin Hart—who couldn't take it any more and left Monash to go to Notre Dame—and from what John Kinsella tells me and others, that there's been a displacement from what was already bad, which was all those horrible Leavisites with their horrible moralisings about literature. They have been replaced by my enemies, what I call the six-fold school of resentment: pseudo-feminists, pseudo-Marxists, not real Marxists and the whole French gang, Foucault, Derrida, Lacan etc., etc., and now of course we have the sexual orientationists, the queer theorists and the closet theorists and I gather that all of that claptrap has replaced Leavisitism. If I was in Australia I wouldn't much like the teaching profession either, if that's all they had. There must be a fair amount of that at Melbourne University?

CA There's certainly some of that.

BLOOM Chris Wallace-Crabbe wouldn't be like that?

CA No, not at all. But he is now at The Australian Centre, a little removed from the department.

BLOOM I don't feel removed from the department at Yale. First of all, because I removed myself. Thirty years ago I left the English department and got reappointed by the 'Corporation of Bloom'. I don't have colleagues and I just give classes. I stopped teaching graduate students a couple of years ago.

CA Why?

BLOOM I decided at my age I was something of a dinosaur and that if I could do anyone any good it would be undergraduates. So I gave two undergraduate seminars each semester: one on Shakespeare and one on the art of reading poetry.

CA I am always interested in the way people say their teaching informs their writing. Do you find that?

BLOOM I think in my case I've written thirty books and I must have written by now 1500 introductions and God knows how many forewords. Everything I have ever written is more a product of teaching than the teaching is a product of the writing. I think I am primarily a teacher and whether I read, write or teach I am doing the same thing.

But I don't agree with the social value—in the immediate social value—of literature or teaching or writing about it. I think that always produces a disaster. Look at the wretchedness of the United States. First we had the counter-culture that has now pretty much become the official culture, which in turn provoked a terrible reaction on the part of the south and the west, and that is why we now have our current political situation. I know there are worse monsters in the world than George W. Bush. There is the dictator of North Korea, there is the President of Iran, there are all these Ayatollahs, and so on and so forth. But of any so-called democratic nation, none of them has a monster as atrocious as George W. Bush. And in the end, I think he is partly the product of the national revulsion against what I would call my former profession.

I would think that in Australia, too, there'll be a backlash and you will get a right wing national regime, unless you have one already. There was a very nice man who I think has now left office. He used to write me very nice letters because he read my books. He was the premier of NSW. He seemed very educated. I think he's left office now.

CA Was it Bob Carr?

BLOOM But I think he's left office now.

CA Yes he has.

BLOOM He is very literate. I think it is a great shame because Australian literature has really been very eminent. You have had Judith Wright, Alec Hope, Les Murray. Murray can be a very difficult personality. We have had our moments, but still he is a very powerful poet. John Kinsella I think is potentially a great poet. To have had a novelist as great as Patrick White and Malouf is very good.

CA I like Malouf. The strange thing is that so many Australians love Tim Winton. He's not one of my favourites.

BLOOM He doesn't do anything for me. Peter Carey is very funny and very good and I like Perlman, this new fellow.

CA He's good.

BLOOM The one called *Seven Types of Ambiguity* is a wonderful novel.

CA I read that when you were teaching at Yale, that you would all read Shakespeare together. I wondered what that entailed because it sounded marvellous.

BLOOM When I am teaching a particular poem or some parts of a passage of Shakespeare, I recite them out loud to the class, usually by memory, and what I am really tempted to do is to ask one of the young women or the young men there to read it out loud, but then they get too shy.

I sometimes tell the students, 'Instead of reading a particular play for next week pick out one of the following groups of passages and sit down in a room by yourself when nobody else is around and just keep reading it out loud to yourself until you really understand it, and you will find that involuntarily you have mostly memorised it'. I tell them to do that with poems like Tennyson's 'Ulysses', Shelley's 'Ode to the West Wind' or Keats' 'To Autumn'. Memorising by rote of course, Cassandra dear, is no good for anyone. But memorising that comes out of deep reading and reading out loud to yourself—so that you are really struggling with something that finds you and won't leave you—that, I think, does a great deal for people. This is because, to a considerable extent, I think the proper use of the best imaginative literature has a great deal to do with memory. (I'm just getting rid of this. [Removes jumper.] I'm on what they call Coumadin, a blood thinner …)

And it's true of all poetry, no matter how deeply reflective. It's astonishing what happens when you recite Tennyson's 'Ulysses' to yourself. I find it enters into my head all the time, sometimes rather sadly:

> Tho' much is taken, much abides; and tho'
> We are not now that which in the old days
> Moved earth and heaven; that which we are, we are;

One equal-temper of heroic hearts,
Made weak by time and fate, but strong in will
To strive, to seek, to find and not to yield.

There's a kind of sadness there. Ulysses, who speaks, is about to go on his last voyage and he is old.

CA It's a very moving piece. Sadly, many students that I teach at university say they were turned off the selection of classics at high school, or that they don't read. How do you get students to love the classics?

BLOOM Well I have noticed through the years at Yale that the students read much less, even when a lot of them are the sons and daughters of my former students, and I get a lot of that now. In one case I even taught the granddaughter of a former student. But that was because in the second year that I taught here, when I wasn't more than twenty-five or so, there were some lady graduate students of twenty-nine or thirty. I was walking out of a class a year ago and I looked at a young lady and I said, 'Why do you look so familiar? I must have taught your mother.' She said, 'No, Professor Bloom, it was my grandmother.' I got so staggered I said, 'Would you mind if I sit down?' I had to absorb that. I said, 'How old is your grandmother?' At that time I was seventy-four and she said, 'She is now seventy-nine, Professor Bloom.' But she was in a graduate class. I gave a graduate class the second year. Sometimes a face skips a generation. She said she doesn't look at all like her mother but she looks exactly like her grandmother. And I thought, quite spookily, that it was her grandmother who had come again.

I've noticed that even at Yale, which is an elitist institution with high admission standards, students come here reading much less than their parents did, and the reason is quite simple. We've turned into a visual culture. As I'm of the old generation, there was no television—there was a radio in the house but I didn't listen much to it and I don't think I went to the movies more than two or three times and the computer didn't exist. I've never learned to type. I have research assistants when I write, who put it on a computer for me, and my wife does the email. I just can't even type. So if you are used to information reaching you visually by the computer, by the television screen, by the motion picture screen, it's difficult to learn how to read deeply and to really be alone with what you are reading. And I think there just aren't enough dedicated teachers in high schools and grade schools, whether in the United States or Australia, to really fight that tendency.

CA Yes, it's a shame. Do you think film adaptations—which are always awful—but do you think that they can positively lead students back to the classics? So they can see *Pride and Prejudice*, because they are visual students who go to movies all the time, that that will lead them back to the classics?

BLOOM The three writers in English who seem to translate well to the screen are Shakespeare, Dickens and Jane Austen, I suppose because all of them abound in fascinating personalities. I don't know what to say about that. I don't think it is a good substitute for reading *Pride and Prejudice* or for reading *Great Expectations* or for reading *Hamlet* or *Henry IV*, to confront it in the film or on the screen instead. I don't know what to say about that, Cassandra dear, but I mean I think we have to face the truth, which is that on a worldwide basis there's now a lot of what you would call semi literacy—people who have been taught to read and who've had full-scale educations, but who are basically not very literate.

CA Yes, it's sad. I wanted to ask you about one of my favourite books, which is the *Stories and Poems for Extremely Intelligent Children of All Ages.*

BLOOM I put that together really as a kind of protest against the *Harry Potter* phenomenon. But on the other hand there is no fighting *Harry Potter*. Rowling is now writing what she says will be the final one in the series. Do you know, and I don't begrudge her this to her, that she is now the richest woman in England? She is richer than Her Majesty Queen Elizabeth II. And I guess she will soon be the richest woman in the world. But it also shows that the debasement of taste is an international phenomenon. The latest *Harry Potter* is read, if that is the right word for it, everywhere.

It instantly gets translated into seventy languages and it is not a literary phenomenon, of course. I'm not sure what we should call it, Cassandra, but it certainly is always there.

CA It has taken hold of people of all ages, too, which is so surprising.

BLOOM I know, I know, child. It's a substitute for reading. I also find Tolkien very badly written, and C. S. Lewis' *Chronicles of Narnia*, which is about to come out as a motion picture. I find it despicable because it is just overt Christian propaganda. And I knew the guy and he was the most dogmatic and aggressive human being I ever knew. The great fantasy writer in English is Lewis Carroll, unless you want to regard Jonathan Swift as a fantasy writer. No one is ever going to do as well as the two Alice books. Beautiful books.

CA They are.

BLOOM Permanent books.

CA Most of the selections in your book are poems and I wondered why so little poetry is read these days and enjoyed?

BLOOM I can't answer the question except to say that really good poetry, not all, but a lot of really good poetry is rather difficult. It depends upon having an inner ear and so few people are now encouraged or trained to read out loud to themselves or to read to other people. But you know Chaucer wrote in order to be read out loud to court audiences, just as Homer wrote to be read out loud, and in Shakespeare, obviously, everything was intended to be read out loud, except for the sonnets. Dickens was a great reader and performer of his own work. He used to give these enormous readings which would go on for hours in which he used to act out all the parts in the novel. That phenomenon we don't have any more—it would exhaust a novelist. I don't exactly see Philip Roth going around giving public readings of his novels. I think he is probably the best novelist we have now in the United States. Poets still give readings; it's become a standard thing, particularly at universities. People have gotten very inhibited about poetry. In fact, you know what cheers me up in the end, Cassandra? I used to be very gloomy about these things but now I'm getting too old to be proper—I'm not as gloomy as I used to be. It seems to me—well look at yourself—in all countries, almost in all social classes, at all ages, there are always going to be real readers who are born. They are people who have something solitary in their souls—people who won't feel that they are themselves, unless they are alone with a book—and a good book, something that speaks to their inner self. *Don Quixote* will always be read, Shakespeare will always be read, Jane Austen will always be read. Some writers perhaps have gotten too difficult. I mean Dante is hardly read anymore even in Italy, because he's too difficult. What will happen to difficult poetry and difficult literature in the future? I don't know? Joyce gambled everything on *Finnegan's Wake* and it's too difficult. Only a few people—I read it again all the time—but only a few people do that and even *Ulysses* now seems too difficult for most readers. I don't know why.

CA People struggle with stream of consciousness.

BLOOM I suppose there is a problem with that, and Proust is not as much read as he should be because he is so funny. The greatest poets of the twentieth century are difficult: Paul Valéry, Yeats with his private mythology, Wallace Stevens in the United States, Hart Crane, who is my favourite poet. He has a very high, powerful driving rhetoric. And with Spanish poets like Luis Cernuda or a Catalan poet like Salvador Espriu, a kind of deep inwardness begins to be cultivated in poetry.

Someone like Alec Hope was a wonderful poet, but very much in the mode of W. H. Auden, who influenced him strongly. It's interesting [poetry], but it's not necessarily the most difficult or complex. In that sense, I suppose, Australia has not produced a sort of difficult, great poet the way the current British poet who matters most, Geoffrey Hill, is difficult, or the way John Ashbery in the United States can be very difficult. I think the most difficult books of highest quality, written by an Australian writer, would be Patrick White's greater books.

CA Do you think that poets and playwrights and novelists make good teachers in universities? Are there many at Yale?

BLOOM John Crowley, who is a very good fantasy writer, who wrote a great book, which I recommend to you, called *Little, Big*. It's a marvellous book. He teaches very well. My old friend, the poet John Hollander, is retired but he occasionally still teaches a course in poetry writing. There's a poet, Louise Glück, here and she is a famously good teacher. I think it just varies from person to person. To a considerable extent, character has a lot to do with it, and learning has a lot to do with it, and a capacity for care has a lot to do with it. But in the end undoubtedly there is an element of personality in it. If you think about the great teachers of history, like Socrates, personality clearly plays a part.

CA Do you think creative writing has a place in an undergraduate or post-graduate degree?

BLOOM Yes, most certainly, most certainly. You might say it helps keep the whole enterprise honest. It is sometimes difficult to get a really good creative writer who teaches, though poets, since they can't really earn livings otherwise, are usually available. Good poets. If novelists are good enough, then they earn enough, so that someone like Philip Roth would never teach—although he did when he was a much younger man.

CA Given your love of Shakespeare, do you go to the theatre very often?

BLOOM No, it is precisely because I love Shakespeare that I don't go to the theatre. We have high concept directors and their concepts don't seem to be Shakespeare's own, so that makes me unhappy. I also have problems with everything else that goes on. It gets very tiresome, child.

CA You re-read Shakespeare and Proust and Swift and White, all of these amazing writers. I wondered how on earth you manage to combine this with teaching and writing and reading new books?

BLOOM I don't sleep. I've always been a bad sleeper. And of course I've had a long time now at seventy-five. I hope I have longer. A pacemaker, I think, is not a serious thing—annoying, but not serious. I always spend my time reading, writing and teaching. I don't do anything else. It's all I've ever done with my life and I'm still fascinated by it.

I get a little sad sometimes because it seems to me there has been a kind of treason of the clerics, as it were, and I don't think it does any good. These people who have politicised study—it not only doesn't do them any good, it doesn't do their students any good. I think it is a lie anyway, because they are not really political. If they really wished to do something about the horrible way in which all societies—western as well as eastern—still treat women, they would be spending their nights in shelters for battered women and for unwed mothers. They would be actively trying to do something politically in local elections, about how badly African Americans and Hispanic Americans are treated—and they're not. I think they're hypocrites. The result of their culture wars has been to frighten large, and admittedly very stupid, portions of American society—the evangelical Christians, so called—the people who throughout the south and the southwest and the Midwest, now dominate American politics.

A democracy, as I understand it, can only function if its citizens are able to think. Thought depends upon memory. What are you going to remember? If what you are going to remember is *Potter* and Stephen King, you haven't got anything to remember. If you have Shakespeare and Jane Austen and George Eliot and Emily Bronte to remember then you've got something to remember and a better chance that you will learn how to think. But the result is that the United States is conducting this hideous and vicious illegal war in Iraq for no reason that I can understand, or that anybody else there would understand. When I was young, the United States was still full of inequalities, particularly in terms of civil rights for the African Americans and Hispanic Americans, but it was relatively speaking, a democracy. Now I would say it's one-third an oligarchy, one-third a plutocracy and one-third a theocracy, which is very bad news indeed.

I suspect that Australian individualism is so fierce that that won't happen. You have a ferocious national temperament as befits so many people who are descended from people who frequently, through no fault of their own, were kicked out of England and sent across as convicts and indentured types, and so forth. So there's a kind of rugged spirit in Australia, which goes with that vast rugged outback of yours, which is mostly a wasteland isn't it? A harsh place, I gather from talking to my friend John Kinsella, but I don't see Australia ever becoming a plutocracy or even an oligarchy or a theocracy. But in this country it has already happened. This is a sick society and it is partly because education has failed here. I don't understand how. It's a disgrace to this university that George Bush got an undergraduate degree here. He is semi-literate at best and he has never in his life read a book all the way through, even when he was a Yale student. He gets his supposed information just from what his aides tell him. I understand that Seymour Hirsch, writing about our Iraqi madness in the *New Yorker* magazine, wrote that Bush tells his friends that he invaded Iraq at the direct suggestion of God himself, of Jesus Christ; that his attempts to bring, what he calls democracy to Iraq, is what Seymour Hirsch rather nicely calls utopianism without information. He has got no information at all; he's got nothing in his head. He certainly can't think. Yet the people of this country didn't really elect him the first time, the election was stolen. But they did elect him the second time.

CA No one could believe it in Australia, either, when he was elected for the second time.

BLOOM He must be the most unpopular person in the world today. He stands for militarism. There was a very great but sinister man in this country—Huey Long—who was Governor of Louisiana and he was assassinated back in 1935. He once said, shortly before his assassination, 'Of course you will have fascism in America but we will call it democracy.' We are sliding towards that now. I hear less and less of protest. I am frequently interviewed over the international phone by Italian, Spanish, Scandinavian and South American journalists and so on and I speak my mind. I say how horrible I find George Bush. How outrageous a policy is which says that all these Mexicans coming into the country are illegal immigrants. That's an outrage. We stole the entire southwest, Texas, New Mexico, Arizona, Utah, all of California. We stole that from the Mexicans. These people are just trying to get back to where their own great-grandparents lived. We put them in jail and call it illegal immigration. I don't know what the future of the United States is. It seems to me that as a nation we are getting stupider every day and less able to see when we are being imposed upon.

CA Well I only have one question, and I guess it's bearing in mind that you have had some health problems in the last couple of years, how does literature console you at times when you are going through a rough patch with your health?

BLOOM Child, I did have a very hard time three and a half to four years ago when I first had a terrible bleeding ulcer. I lost six pints of blood. I was a total of seven weeks in hospital because they had to do an open-heart three-way by-pass and the current problem is not serious compared to that, it is just putting in a pacemaker …

CA No, a pacemaker is not that serious. How does literature get you through?

BLOOM I recited poems. I recited poems to myself out loud all of the time if I was alone. If people were nearby and it would bother them I just recited them to myself. I know practically all the poetry I have ever cared for, by heart. So I just recite it to myself. And of course there's my wife. We've been married for forty-eight years.

CA And you have a wonderful relationship.

BLOOM A wonderful relationship. She is the boss. It's better that way. I think in the western world—and I think this is what Shakespeare teaches us—really superior women are all, in a sense, condemned to marry down. There are a few exceptions.

I am often asked if I was bothered by Bloom referring to me as 'my child' in this interview. I think it is a strange question. I found it endearing and felt it was an indication of the age difference between us. At the end of the interview he called me a cab, helped me back into my pink parka and kissed me on the top of the head. I felt like a favourite grandchild and left hoping one day I might return to his kitchen and discuss Shakespeare and poetry with him.

'I am interested in extraordinary moments' *James Green*

There is something wonderfully erudite about Jim Green. He is quietly compelling; a natural storyteller. I read his book, Death in the Haymarket (2006), about the Haymarket Massacre in Chicago and was drawn to the unique style and re-telling of history that Jim had created. I had read about the riot in Haymarket Square in history textbooks, but it wasn't until I read Jim's book that it really came to life for me; it was only then that I understood the way in which this moment was an important turning point in history.

Green is currently professor of history and labor studies at The University of Massachusetts, but before he became an academic, he worked on Senator McCarthy's 1968 presidential campaign, was a labor activist and wrote for Radical America, among other things. Perhaps, most interestingly, he taught leadership training workshops for unions. His connection with the United Mine Workers of America is well documented. Green lectured in the Labor and Worklife program at Harvard Law School, was a Fulbright scholar and taught at the University of Genoa, in Italy. In 2009 he was awarded the Sol Stetin Award for Labor History.

I had arranged to meet Jim at the JFK museum. He teaches at UMass, just a short shuttle bus ride from the museum. But, more importantly, I had read that Jim was inspired by JFK to study history and politics, so it was fitting that the interview took place there. I wish I could have interviewed him in the glass pavilion at the museum with the American flag soaring overhead and JFK quotations adorning the walls, but it is more of a silent space. In many ways, this room reminds me of Jim—quietly confident and impressive. I think that Jim would have made a great president; when I talked to him, I felt like I was talking to a leader. And it didn't hurt that, like Kennedy, he cut a fine figure!

In the end, we met in the light-filled museum café and talked as people moved from the exhibits to filling up on bowls of clam chowder or munching on homemade cake while they chatted about the Kennedy legacy. That afternoon, Kennedy and Green were 'in the air'.

CA I wanted to start with JFK, since we are at the JFK museum. I read an article where you said you found him inspiring and that he was one of your early heroes. Also, heroes and the discussion of a hero, seem to be a little out of fashion at the moment, people prefer to discuss significant periods of time or an event. Is it important to come back to this idea of a hero or not?

GREEN That's a good question. As a boy studying history when Kennedy became president—and these photographs, here, remind me of the excitement when he visited the town where I was a student at school—it was definitely a 'hero worship' kind of thing. It extended back in my reading to Arthur Schlesinger Jnr., who was Kennedy's intellectual adviser; to reading Schlesinger's heroisation of FDR; to [Andrew] Jackson and growing up in Illinois and all the heroism about Lincoln. So I certainly grew up with it and the 'Great Man' had a very compelling affect on me, so much so that it made me interested in becoming a politician, which I pursued by going to Washington for a couple of summers and working with a US senator as an intern.

But then the war in Vietnam came along and I think for my generation, without being hyperbolic, that changed everything in some ways. It certainly made us question the cult of the hero because of course there was Kennedy and even Johnson—I was very enthusiastic about Johnson in '64. He was running against Barry Goldwater, he was going to save us from nuclear war because Goldwater was going to blow up the Soviet Union. So in a way, Johnson was a kind of unlikely hero, too. But by the end of the sixties these kinds of figures had been discredited by events and so it all made us look back—I remember reading Howard Zinn on FDR, Hofstadter on *The American Political Tradition*, there was all this debunking.

On the other hand, I will say, we had Robert F. Kennedy and Martin Luther King and Malcolm X and César Chávez, and so I think they were kind of our surrogate heroes. It never really disappeared and I can't say that it is absent from my work even now. There are certain people who play heroic roles on the stage in history and some of these people were like that – especially when they are tragic heroes. So even though I politically distance myself from that heroic presidency, I haven't completely escaped the lure of men in politics (and let's be honest, it is 'men'), men in power or men out of power but speaking the truth to power, people like King, so on and so forth. This cuts across the grain of my own work as a social historian, which is not to try to elevate individuals but to demonstrate the power of movements.

CA What do you think are the advantages and disadvantages of an historian working at a university?

GREEN I have had a peculiarly good experience here [at UMass]. I say peculiarly because some people with my politics have really struggled with the academy in a sense. In the academy many of them have been unable to continue their work.

I had a mixed experience. In my first job I found that my activism and my career were not compatible. I was 'let go', as they say. I can't prove that it was because of my political activity but I certainly thought so at the time. In any case, I found myself here, at the University of Massachusetts, in an alternative college, which was sort of composed of faculty like me. So in some ways my activism—strangely because this is not the case in academia at all as a rule—proved to be an asset. It is one of the reasons I was hired here. Throughout my career here, I have been able to work with one foot in each world: professional scholarship with professional association and the Labor movement and community groups. However, this has become less so as I have become more involved in writing because there are only so many meetings you can go to when you are trying to write a book! But I have been very lucky, I would say, and I have to give a lot of credit to this institution for creating the space and the support. My work is highly valued here by people of all levels at the university and there are no apologies, whether the things I do are political or not.

CA What do you think are the responsibilities of the public intellectual?

GREEN The most difficult thing—I have tried to work as an intellectual with the Labor movement, which has always been a difficult task—is the fact that you are an outsider, that's my public. And then the public beyond that is the public that thinks unions are terrible and should be done away with. So, that larger public is easier to deal with, I can say. But within the Labor Union community as a public, I think my responsibilities are to be part of that movement to voice principles and objectives but at the same time tell the truth. To tell you the truth that has been difficult, at times, to be the critic at the same time that you are trying to be the ally. People don't understand that.

CA Does a Labor history professor find it difficult to connect with Labor activists because universities are considered elitist and you are, therefore, the enemy?

GREEN That certainly was true, initially, in the 1980s when I was beginning. I wouldn't say the union people were wrong, that is to say I have come from a world of privilege and a certain kind of verbal facility and I think they resented it, on the one hand, and found it threatening and easy to dismiss. Except for their own people who had some connection to university, they had never had to deal with someone like me on a direct basis. And that was an icy period of almost ten years where I was at odds with the top people who came out of the defence industry. They were Cold War people and to be fair for them—which is easier for me to do now—they didn't see any possible contribution that I could make. I was just this guy who was in some ways a critic. What broke that log jam was that my own students were part of the Labor movement and they valued my work, precisely because I was intellectual and precisely because I was critical and because I could lecture and write and all the things that officials found objectionable or even threatening, that was what they wanted.

When I flatter myself, I'd like to think that I was more than just a professor to them; that I was an ally of theirs, a comrade, someone who was more than their professor. But that is presumptuous and you would have to talk to them. My hope was that I could carve out a role for them that would mean that I would continue to contribute what I had to, but without seeming like I was coming from the Ivory Tower.

CA Do you have to have working class credentials to write Labor history?

GREEN There are a lot of working class people who have made their way into academic life and they do have credentials. I mean, I wouldn't say that I was completely lacking in credentials, I guess I would say that I grew up middle class. My father was a high school teacher and, certainly, in our community there was a real difference, perceptually, in terms of who he was—a teacher who went to school and wore a coat and tie—I was aware of that. However, I lived in a company house and we lived around factory workers. I walked to school every day by a glass furnace and I was surrounded by immigrants and Catholics. All these things made it a world that wasn't strange to me. It wasn't like I was coming from an elite background. In fact, I think a lot of my comfort zone—because you can feel very uncomfortable if you are from a privileged background, being with people who aren't—comes from being from that kind of small town. There were no racial distinctions to speak of and it wasn't very class segregated. And growing up Catholic, there was this sense that this was not the church of the elite. Some of the people in your parish were successful businessmen, maybe a lawyer or two, but everyone else were just ordinary people.

When I talk to the guys from over here, they are all Irish Catholics, there is something very easy about it and I think that if I was Jewish or Episcopalian, it might be different. I just feel comfortable around them, I don't feel out of place even though my father wasn't a factory worker – my grandfather was a factory worker. It is partly an American thing – there are all these ways in which people can move – (it's much easier for a white male) – in and out of different social strata. I have even found myself comfortable among black folks, although I would say that mostly the black people that I work with are students or activists or intellectuals, but I feel comfortable with them as well. It is part of the work. There are public intellectuals for whom that is not crucial. It's about Noam Chomsky's ideas, it is not about whether you want to go and have a beer with him or not; it's irrelevant. But that's not true for me. A lot of my work is face to face, building credibility, building relationships, not writing a book about American imperialism.

CA You talk about your classes with trade unionists and ask your students to explore current ideas as well as looking at the past.

How important is a balance of looking at 'now' and looking at the past?

GREEN I have always found the students focussed entirely on the present. They will look at the historical situation and say, 'that's exactly, the way it is now. The rich get richer and the poor get poorer. People are greedy …' I always struggle, quite a bit, to acknowledge the resonance of the past in the present. It is still there, and in fact when people read this book [*Death in the Haymarket*] they often talk about capitalism; what it was then and what it is now and how immigrants have to deal with it. So I am happy that people see, 120 years ago, certain pieces, problems and tendencies that we are still struggling with today. But I am an intellectual academic person in the sense that it is not just about what the past can tell us about what to do – because it often really can't do that. It is more a way of thinking about society, of thinking about politics, of thinking about power, about how people who are powerless and in this story [Haymarket], find themselves empowered. I think that the problem with relating everything to the present is you don't necessarily see that. A lot of people ask me about this May Day stuff, and I say, 'Maybe, there certainly is that kind of feeling that existed then.' But what happens will be an entirely different script from what happened then. But the mood; the temper; the feeling of being in the streets; the feeling of solidarity; the feeling of taking on the US congress; all these things were very much present in 1886.

I am interested in those extraordinary moments like in 1968, when people felt they could turn the world upside down. Even though you then have the grimmer obligation to explain why that didn't happen—and this in some ways can be discouraging or tragic that this promise wasn't realised—that is part of the job as well. I mean, I could have just made it into a celebration, when in fact, you have to say, it was kind of a disaster.

CA History books can be dry but you have a wonderful prose style, which is fluent and has flair. How important is it to be able to write history in a compelling way?

GREEN Let me ask you a question and then I will answer yours. Mostly people have responded the way you have. There have been a variety of readers and I am very pleased about it, and they are not just university people. A couple of people have said that it takes too long to get through the history of Chicago, to get to the action. Is that what you found?

CA No, because I don't know very much about Chicago, so I found the history interesting as well. It framed the narrative for me. Maybe because I am from Australia, I found it all really new and exciting, but I didn't find it took too long to get to the action.

GREEN Good. I felt I needed to do that even though it was harder to write the framework in a compelling narrative – I had to be very creative about the way I constructed those early chapters.

CA It's important to set the scene …

GREEN Yes, exactly. I wanted the reader to ask, 'Why Chicago?' and be able to answer that question. So your question is really crucial to me and this question is what led me to turn my attention, and frankly, a lot of my time, towards writing. At this point in my life I thought, 'Well, I get two to three emails every day about things that are going on.' I've got a call I have to return now about a union that is in the final stages of negotiation with a human service agency that is actually caring for my daughter and they want me to come out, in public, and they want me to help them with the negotiations. I do as many things of these things as I can, but in the last three years, I have done fewer.

When I had a chance to write this book, I said to my editor, 'This story has been told many times, but I think I have told it differently.' And he said, 'Yes, it's all in the writing.' And I came to believe that because as a radical Left intellectual, for many, many years, I didn't make [my prose style] the centre of my attention. I was always a naturally good writer but it was about proving or disproving something; providing some knowledge that people didn't have or trying completely to change how people thought about class consciousness; all these big projects. So the writing was just a means to an end. I've come to realise that if I want to reach a larger public—and this book has done that—it has to be written in a way that people will find engaging at a human level. There is no Theory in there, except very deep, beneath the structure, the narrative is there – but you would never think, 'He is giving me a lesson in Theory.'

CA In Australia, people are less inclined to be members of unions now. Do you think it is a generational thing or do you think they will perhaps die out?

GREEN That seems to be happening in the private sector. I have spent my life studying Labor history, so there may be something cyclical about this and something generational. This is what people would have said about the 1920s in the United States, they don't care—particularly all the new immigrants, so they are afraid or they don't care—because the economy was doing well, the republicans were ruling the roost, because it was the land of individual opportunity, all those things. Unions were in much worse shape than they are now. Of course, the crisis came and people had no protection, so then all of a sudden you get a new Labor movement – I'm simplifying this enormously because it took organisers to make that happen. I don't know if it will happen in my lifetime—I hope it does—but I can imagine that happening.

You look at what people are up against in terms of housing costs, lack of health care, inability to have children, all these kinds of things right now. If you talked to workers I would say 7 out of 10 of them would say things are really bad. And if you asked them if they wanted to join a union, they would say, 'What difference would that make?' when, in fact, it would. Joining a union in most parts of the United States, except the South, is just an obvious thing to do. My sister, who is a teacher in Illinois, was in a school district where the teachers decided that they didn't want the union. Now she is in the city and they belong to a union and her salary has quadrupled because of the union contracts. People in the public sector understand that and people in the building trades. If you talk to people who are willing to become apprentices, there is a big advantage to being in the union. I can't imagine how you would successfully unionise Burger King, McDonald's and Walmart. And it has to do with the attitudes of the workers who might, in fact, like to have protection and better wages but they don't see any connection between their problems and some sort of collective solution. I used to blame it on the unions but I actually think they are out there doing a pretty good job of trying to get the message out. It is not as though people have never heard of unions, some people haven't, but I think it will probably get worse before it gets better in terms of numbers. It may also be that we are at a point in history where the trade union idea is almost two hundred years old and it began with a very, very limited concept of what a union was – which is a very small group of people doing the same kind of jobs for their whole lives. That works extremely well, it works for us here at the university where everybody here belongs to the union. But for many workers, it simply may no longer be a practical solution to their problems. Take, for instance, health care. We thought, we'll join a union and get health care, but now even GM is saying, 'we can't afford it.' So that's not the solution any more. So there has to be national health care as a solution to that and in a way, the unions are not part of the solution. However, they are part of the problem as they have created a protective sphere for their members—not at the expense of other people—but without access for other people. So a lot of the things that unions fought for—the eight hour day which eventually became something that everyone except agricultural workers were supposed to have—was achieved for people whether they were in the union or not. And in a way, that is the way it should be. The numbers of members of unions are not so important to me as whether people have healthy, safe lives, free from abuse; have some security; have some healthcare. What you miss without the union would be a sense of democracy, of having some say about your work place. That could still be what people want. The polls show that the majority say if they had the opportunity to have a say in their work environment and have a voice, they would want it. But that is a long way from there to saying, 'And I would go out and I would risk my job.'

CA I know you have made films and I have shown some of them in my lectures. Do you use films in your lectures?

GREEN I use documentary film and some feature film in my lectures. It is always hard when you teach to fit films into a context. I don't like showing clips but I do use all those films from the Great Depression.

CA They are great films! You have been travelling around speaking to people. Has that been rewarding?

GREEN It's been great. When you write a book you hope you will be able to talk to people about it and I have made about twenty public appearances and fifteen interviews like this. On the one hand, it is sometimes somewhat limited to speak about what happened—telling the story—but whenever we get into Q and A, which is a lot of the time, something good always comes out of it.

'My history is a tile in a mosaic' *Jim Cullen*

Jim Cullen is dynamic. He is a scholar who is so rigorously intelligent that he can, and does, write about complex concepts in an accessible manner. His blog at American History Now *is compulsive reading. Reviews of books, many on American history, are juxtaposed with discussions of singers and actors, from Taylor Swift to Daniel Day-Lewis. Nothing escapes Jim's attention! He can discuss Obama's presidency on the one hand and review* Gangs of New York *on the other. The first time I met Jim, he was conducting a seminar with a group of Australian students studying American history. Students asked him questions and he offered lightning fast responses, often turning the tables and asking students their views; challenging them and asking them to re-think their responses. They couldn't keep up, just as I can't keep up with his incredible publishing schedule. He recently published,* Sensing the Past: Hollywood Stars and Historical Visions, *and his next book,* Stages, Pages and Screens: A Short History of the Modern Media *is forthcoming from Wiley Blackwell. In addition to that, he seems to publish something new on his blog about every twelve hours!*

Cullen was born in Queens, New York, and attended public schools on Long Island. He received his BA in English from Tufts University, and his A.M and PhD degrees in American Civilization from Brown University. He has taught at a number of colleges and universities, including Harvard and Brown. He is currently a teacher, and serves on the Board of the Trustees, at the Ethical Culture Fieldston School in New York City. He is married to historian Lyde Cullen Sizer and has four children. Cullen is the leading expert on the American Dream, with the publication of an incredible number of books in American history such as: The American Dream: A Short History of an Idea that Shaped a Nation, Born in the U.S.A.: Bruce Springsteen and the American tradition *and* Restless in the Promised Land: Catholics and the American Dream. *His specialisation in American Civilisation makes him a scholar with a broad view of history and an incredible range of knowledge. This substantiates his claim that he is a lumper; he prioritizes 'the big picture' and this encompasses far ranging topics such as the American presidents, the civil war, Bruce Springsteen, Ralph Waldo Emerson, John Steinbeck and of course, the American Dream and the way it relates to struggles over labor.*

In many ways it is his expansive and far reaching understanding of the American Dream that ties all of his interests together. Cullen talks about the Dream both poetically and wistfully. The Dream is subtle and malleable, everyone's dream is different and yet everyone has a dream. This can be difficult for Australian students to come to grips with, but Cullen reminds them that even though many American Dreams are not realized, having a dream is its own reward. Cullen loves popular culture and his discussions are always peppered with relevant and current examples from the contemporary world.

I interviewed him in an empty classroom at the Fashion Institute of Technology in New York. He was speaking to another group of students after our interview in the common room. He sat at a bare table, ubiquitous cap on his head, and was incredibly generous with his answers and his time. He is still my favourite lumper!

CA Do you think teaching makes you a better writer?

CULLEN I think it does. It is an important reality check in two ways. The first is that you have a sample audience on which to plant an idea and secondly it's a way of getting ideas from people. And I, as a high school teacher with students, do not have a lot of experience working with writers, I show them a lot of my own work; I circulate my work. A lot of my work in recent years has increasingly been focused on students as an audience, not necessarily writing text books but thinking about a younger generation of people; how they're inclined to think about things and how one might best address them. The last couple of books I have done in particular have been generated as books in which I have thought about adolescents and young adults as my primary audience.

CA Can you tell me a little bit about American students and teaching?

CULLEN I've taught undergraduates, I've taught graduate students, I've taught adult students and I've taught high school students. In one sense there is no difference. The real difference is the content level and that way in which you teach differently to a beginner than you do to someone who is immersed in a discourse. But there is a particular dimension, I think, in talking to younger people. First of all, you are typically introducing them to all kinds of things, not just the subject. For example, when I am talking about westward expansion of the United States I often talk about real estate business and I realise that many of these people have never owned a property and don't know what it means to have a mortgage and to have to pay things off. So you have to think about those kinds of life skills—elementary lessons—in order to understand the context. Second, of course, is the dimension of memory, what these people know or don't know. I am very aware that the students I'm going to be teaching in the fall were born circa 1990, that is, after the Berlin wall came down. This is a reasonably shocking sort of framework within which to work and, of course, you have to talk to people differently. I am finishing a project where I start with Thomas Jefferson and I end with George Bush. With Jefferson, of course, you have to provide all kinds of background information, but with Bush it would be deadly to provide background information. People don't need to know about war on terror or the war in Iraq, they know that all too well. So the act of calibration is such an important part of teaching and such an important part of writing.

CA It can be strange teaching students about 9/11 and asking them what they were doing when the two towers collapsed—much like people used to ask what people were doing when JFK was shot—because students now would have been very young and probably sleeping and so it doesn't have the same impact. Do you teach your students about 9/11?

CULLEN I do, and of course I teach in New York City where it happened. I teach students whose families were touched by it and I teach at a school where people were lost. That adds a very powerful dimension to things, so much so that I've had to walk a line, even making sure I talk to a kid and let him know, 'Hey, we're going to talk about this thing, you might not want to be here.' Interestingly enough, in the case I'm thinking of, the student was quite interested in staying and quite vocal about it—but that's not something you can take for granted, so there are sensitivities that you have to take into account. Part of the problem with 9/11 and part of the problem of history, generally, is to make people think hard about the ways in which the past both is, and isn't, like the present. And I think that the instinct a lot of people have—which is not a bad instinct, and in many cases it is a correct instinct—is to say that this is just like what happened before. So they say, 'this is just like Pearl Harbour' or, 'this is just like the cold war', but in fact it's not. As much as historical judgement is about trying to get people to forge connections, it is also about appreciating the differences. That, I find, is a big part of my job as a writer and a teacher. I strive to complicate texture; to make people aware of the ways things are not alike, as well as the way they are alike.

CA Kenneth T. Jackson has stated that history is in trouble because in secondary schools in America, teachers are employed to teach social studies and may not have studied history and that is detrimental to fostering a love of history. Is this an accurate picture of secondary school teachers in America? In Australia we have the study of SOSE in secondary schools which couples geography with history asking the teacher to diversify their specialist area. Is this a good idea?

CULLEN I'm sure there is some truth to what Jackson is saying, and clearly people who teach social studies, per se, don't have quite the same commitment as an historian—they can't. But, of course, their problems are much bigger than the vicissitudes of a particularly visionary discourse. Often, or not, they are worried about their class size; they're worried about attendance; they're worried about disciplinary problems; they're worried about all kinds of things, whether they want to be or not. In some ways professors like Kenneth Jackson, for whom I have enormous regard, really are in an ivory tower—especially at a place like Columbia because, of course, in a lot of colleges and universities, many of these issues pertain to them as well. In my mind, the challenges of teaching history well, have less to do with the integrity of the historical enterprise, less about the quality of archival research and the tenor of the sources and the kinds of skills—frankly— that a lot academic historians have lost sight of. These include: story telling; organising information in a compelling way; bringing some of the arts of theatre, as well as the arts of history, to bear on a room. Those things are as likely as not to make the experience of learning memorable for people, as it is the unteachable quality of the historical arguments.

CA How do you find time to write with the demands of teaching?

CULLEN I wish I had a good answer for you; it's a good question. For example, I was supposed to be working on the book I am just finishing over the summer, but I ended up working on it over the course of the school year, which a lot of people don't do. I see this less in a boasting way—in fact I have real questions about myself, and you can talk to my wife and children about the costs of doing this. I really don't want to toot my own horn because I am not entirely sure it is a great thing. In some sense—and this really brings me to the heart of the answer—I think for a lot of us, certainly myself, it doesn't come from some sort of rational place, even some sort of career place. It's an itch that you cure by scratching a pen. It's something that you are compelled to do. I don't think there is any other reason to do it—I was going to say any other *good* reason to do it—but I'm not sure my reasoning is altogether good.

CA With your style and the flow and the way your books are accessible to a wide range of people, have you ever thought of writing fiction?

CULLEN I've tried! I've tried and I know that there are some people who really can do both, but I do have this idea that fiction and non-fiction really are separate enterprises and that they require different skill sets. For example, the American historian David Potter has said that there are two paths for historians: there are lumpers and there are splitters. I'm a lumper, myself, and my wife is a splitter—that's why I think it works. I have this idea of fiction writers—I don't know if that taxonomy works—but the point is, that they have a different DNA, I think; a different way of approaching things. In my limited experience in dealing with people who I really think of as artists, they have what seems to be a kind of healthy scepticism about the kind of analytic tools that a non-fiction writer brings to bear on his or her work. I think they are afraid it is going to complicate or conflict their methodology—in fact, even a word like 'methodology' probably gives some fiction writers the freaks. I have tried to do it and, of course, I really do believe that history is finally an imaginative act, but I guess I have too much respect for fiction writers to think that I ever could be one.

CA You often concentrate on people in American history like Bruce Springsteen and Ronald Reagan. Is it through people rather than through periods of time that we learn about history?

CULLEN Well, you know, history in the last 30 years in the United States has been about process, not people, and there's some very, very good reasons for that. But it's hard to tell a good story about a process—it's possible to do and there are people who have done it—but, again, if you are talking with a bunch of sixteen year-olds, and you focus on industrialisation and any kind of 'tion' word, you're going to have to look at getting it out of the gate to begin with. However, if you can hang it on something, even an object like the Erie canal, you're going to get a hell of a lot more mileage than you are if you are talking about the state of the economy and the legislative structure of the New York assembly that might make that possible.

Instead, I think, you've got to work with a figure like DeWitt Clinton, who of course is not going to give you the whole story, you're going to distort the story by hanging it on such a person. But there is no sort of pure place from which to tell any story, anyway. So, if you accept that at the outset and you have some sort of commitment to the truth—a commitment which may be moral as much as it is factual—you just have to do the best you can with what you've got to work with. And what you have to work with is, as often as not, an audience, as it is a subject.

CA How else do you make students interested in the past? I've heard that you use pop. culture and film.

CULLEN In some sense that's how I began my work or career. You see I calculated that was the way 'in'. It still is. I'm going to be teaching 'The World Since 1940' this fall and I'm going to begin with a Bruce Springsteen song about a man at a checkpoint in Iraq seeing the car coming and not being sure whether it's a friend or a foe. And that kind of traumatic situation is a better way to begin than saying: 'In 1945 the world was divided between two great powers.' I feel that I use pop. culture not simply because it is a useful tactic, but it also reflects my own personal and ideological commitments. I come out of a working class childhood. I did not have a lot of books around the house growing up. I had television shows, I had movies and that's how I initially made sense of the world. I have a commitment to the printed word but I'm not one of those people who doesn't let my children watch television. I think of that as an elitist position on some level, even though I know television does things to your brain differently than reading does things to your brain—and not always good things. So the reason that I have worked a lot with popular culture reflects my background but it also reflects my belief in the best way to reach students—and of course, that's where I learn a lot, too. I didn't know anything about hip hop, for example, until I met these students, because I am the wrong size and colour and age.

CA What responsibilities do you feel you have in regards to your students and the teaching of history?

CULLEN Well I'm very aware, especially at the school where I teach, that I am dealing with the next generation of American leadership and I'm hoping that they are going to be responsible, thoughtful people. And so, in some sense, the question is not so much about my fidelity to the past but rather my fidelity as a teacher and what I might be able to give these people to equip them to become thoughtful, responsible people. Maybe by my doing well by them, they can do well by others. As Thomas Jefferson says, 'The earth belongs to the living.' History is for the living too, for better or worse.

CA You work at a school [Ethical Culture Fieldston School] which seems very privileged. How do you feel about this given that the American Dream is built on the idea of the equality of education?

CULLEN That is a fair question, and it is a question that would have to come up a lot for any person who wanted to do anything resembling a decent job—broadly construed. The school where I teach is certainly a place of privilege and has been for some time. It also has, like many elite schools in the United States, a real commitment to diversity by providing opportunity. Sometimes this diversity, this opportunity, has a kind of manicured quality to it, which doesn't always necessarily reflect the realities of American demography. In fact, insofar as there is equality of opportunity in the United States anymore—and I really do think it is diminishing—education remains. I certainly teach more than a few people from modest backgrounds. And of course they're the people, in some sense, I have the greatest investment in, having come from such a background myself. Of course, we all have an investment; we all want to believe that the enterprise we are engaged in has some sort of legitimacy. That said, rich people need help, too, and in some sense rich people need help so that they can help others. The fact that I teach at a school called The Ethical Culture Fieldston School sets us up for a lot of stickers, a lot of griping, a lot of accurate complaints of democracy. But without some faith in the validity in the enterprise you are doing, then you can't really function—and of course, we all do, really, want to function.

CA Was your dad a fireman? Does it give you more credibility to talk about working class issues?

CULLEN

The question of class is always complicated. How do you define it and can you take the boy out of poverty or the poverty out of the boy? I don't want to make any false claims from my own background. I never really had any privation to speak of. The principle form of privilege I enjoy is through education. I feel like one of the things I give my students, not so much what I get in return, but what I give them, is my father's voice. They need to hear him and therefore I really sort of channel him regularly. They hear what a white, working class conservative has to say. They hear the not so nice things he said as well as the real challenges and the real questions he has for them. I think that this is probably one of the most important things I bring to the table at my school—not my mastery of the subject, not my hoped for decency as a human being—my history, and that history is a tile in a mosaic that they are all going to build.

CA Your books are so patriotic and get to the heart of America. This seems to be your quest. Have you ever thought of deviating from this topic of America?

CULLEN As I get older and as I hopefully learn a little bit more, in some ways, I become more and more aware of the ways in which the United States is not, in fact, exceptional. I become aware of the fact that one can speak, for example, of a Roman dream of citizenship and upward mobility, although no-one ever does. This Roman dream is not, in the end, that different from the American dream in terms of ethnic diversity, upward mobility, a sense of citizenship and so on. I am aware, of course, that there are real parallels to be made between, for example, the American experience and the Oceanic experience in terms of colonialism and even things like the ethnic composition and race relations and so on. This does intrigue me more and more as time goes on and I'm also more and more aware of the ways in which globalisation in a contemporary context both is and is not the same as Americanisation. Of course, it is my fate to be born at a time of a widely perceived American decline and the notion that something is going to follow, perhaps inevitably, makes one think about something that comes before.

CA I read your article on Vietnam ['Vietnam War is History, Not Current Events for U.S Teens', *Voice of America*, 28 April 2005. http://www.politicsol.com/news/2005/04-28-vietnam-war-is-history-not-current-events-for-us-teens.html] and making it relevant to students. It was a great article and two students discussed their reactions to the war. You mentioned Bruce Springsteen in the article and the 9/11 album [*The Rising*, Sony, 2002.] What do you think of it? Why is Bruce such an important person to you? [Cullen has written *Born in the USA: Bruce Springsteen and the American Tradition*, Harper Collins, 1997].

CULLEN I think of Bruce Springsteen as someone who puts the best face on America, especially when the rest of the world has some serious questions about the United States. He embodies many of the values that all Americans honour: values like hard work; a commitment to family and friends that is as much about deeds as words; a love of country that recognises failure as well as honours success, these kinds of things. And I think that one of the things that Springsteen does very well is that he has a real sense of history and his music is quite resonant. I'm teaching a course to adults right now at an arts college and I'm going to teach a class on *The Rising*. Most people I will deal with are a little older and they really did live through 9/11. They also lived through a bunch of other things and so, even though many of these people are a generation or two even older than Springsteen himself, there is an opportunity to kind of cut across generations. I'll be interested to see to what degree that actually works.

CA It will be interesting to see how familiar they are with the CD. I'm not sure how well it was received in America but it didn't really have a huge market in Australia, and you can understand why.

CULLEN It was Springsteen's first record with the E Street band for about twenty years. It charted relatively well, but it was not a major record in terms of its commercial impact. I think Springsteen's influence now is a little bit more diffuse than that. I was listening to a very popular radio show in the United States called 'The Prairie Home Companion' which is all sort of old American music, sort of classic American, gospel and country music and—I don't know what you call it—a hillbilly outfit doing a very obscure Springsteen song, actually from *Devils and Dust* [Columbia records 2005] It sounded like it could have been recorded in the 1930s. So I think the Springsteen legacy may now be as an iconic figure. You know Woody Guthrie or Frank Sinatra without necessarily knowing their music, although some people certainly do. Some people know virtually nothing but they know who those people are, they know what they stand for and I think that's probably where Springsteen is headed in terms of his iconography in American culture.

CA Is reading under threat? Do students still read or is PlayStation taking over?

CULLEN I'm sure that a lot of Greek poets were disappointed by the decline of the oral tradition and confused by people's new-fangled commitment to papyrus. Media has changed and all media has costs and benefits. There's no question, for example, that the students I teach have a much more sharply attuned visual sense than I do. I think their ability to decode a movie is much more natural and much less conscious than my own process was—so in that sense I don't want to be a naysayer or a Luddite. I think of reading like being in good physical shape. When you are in good shape, you don't break a sweat doing certain tasks. I don't regard reading one hundred pages or reading a book in a day or two to be a big deal. I've never regarded reading a book or two in a month or a summer as a big deal and, you know, sometimes that's their loss as much as it is our loss. I am a child of the word and I will die a child of the word and I am grateful for what it has given me. However, I don't assume that everyone needs to be a child of the word to have a long and fruitful life. I've seen too many people who don't and haven't.

CA Do you need an ego to stay in the publication industry? How do you deal with negative reviews and where do you get your strength from?

CULLEN I find that in order to write a book, you certainly need the sustaining illusion that what you are doing is good. Often, I never feel better about anything I've written in the heated aftermath than in the middle of writing it. Later I'll rip it up or throw it out or more affectionately say, 'that wasn't a bad piece of work', but I think in that moment you have to sort of believe in what you are doing. You also have to believe that there is going to be another one; that if you don't get it right, now, maybe you'll get it right later. At some point, you come up for air, you look back and realise that you have produced a body of work and you can take comfort in that. You know you're not perfect and you know that even when you do good work it's not necessarily going to be recognised. You know, I think that it is difficult to believe that there is some kind of justice about all of this, people who write lousy books get recognised, people who write great books don't. We are never as good as we want to be; we are never as bad as we think. In the end it has to come from that internal place, that itch—that's the only thing that really will keep you going.

'I like cities and don't like fishing' *Kenneth T. Jackson*

To an Australian ear, Kenneth T. Jackson has a wonderful Southern drawl—which is not what you expect from the leading expert on New York—unless you know that he was born in Memphis, Tennessee. I have been interested in Jackson ever since watching Ric Burns' New York: A Documentary Film. *I remember him talking about the history of the New York subway and the original 30-mile ride that only cost a nickel. Jackson could even make mass transit interesting.*

Jackson is currently director of the Herbert H. Lehman Center for American History and the Jacques Barzun Professor of History and Social Sciences at Columbia University. His books, Cities in American History *(1972) and* Crabgrass Frontier: The Suburbanization of the United States *(1985), are classic texts that showcase Jackson's engaging writing style and all-encompassing knowledge of the wonder of cities. His books ooze the same kind of confidence that Jackson, himself, exhibits as he walks around the campus at Columbia. People are drawn to him and students go out of their way to greet him. He acknowledges them with a nod, a wave or a smile.*

One of his many legacies is his annual, late night, bike ride through New York with huge numbers of students in tow. This event is part of his subject, 'The History of the City of New York'. He has been conducting this ride for 37 years and I would love to do it one day, if I could sneakily tail his students. Riding into Times Square and cycling to the romantic Brooklyn Promenade with a bunch of other New York enthusiasts sounds wonderful. And who else is better qualified to show you around New York? Jackson has edited three of the most important books on New York: The Encyclopedia of New York *(1995),* Empire City *(2002) with David Dunbar,* and Robert Moses and the Modern City: The Transformation of New York *(2007) with Hilary Ballon.*

I interviewed Jackson in a classroom at Columbia University. We sat on chairs on a raised platform at the front of the room. He is a busy man and it seemed as if, perhaps, he had done this one too many times. However, he was gracious and as the interview progressed he appeared to become more interested in the questions and offered some rousing responses.

His personal assistant was able to anticipate his needs and offered him, at various points, a drink of cola, a pen and, most importantly, acted as his timekeeper. When she told me that my time was up, I left Columbia and took a ride on the subway. I sat there, marvelling at Jackson's foresight; he really does love New York.

CA You were born in Memphis, Tennessee and completed your PhD at the University of Chicago, how did you develop your love of New York?

JACKSON Well, I was trained as an urban historian and so I thought it would be useful to live in New York. I grew up in a relatively small city and so I thought that if I was going to spend my life doing this, I should know what big cities are like. And so I came here, in part, as a career move. I thought I would be here for a few years and it would help me. I think it is true that being in New York helps you understand inner cities. I don't know what I think it gives people, but I do think it gives people something in the United States.

But another thing is, I think it is inside you. My mother loved cities and so it's like if you like liver or cornbread or whatever—I like cities and don't like fishing. And New York agrees with me. I love the diversity and stuff like that. I think it is less an accident of where you were born as an accident of genes. I don't know the answer to that.

CA Many historians choose not to work in universities or to be 'research-only' academics and do not teach. Why is teaching important to you?

JACKSON For most Americans, if you are going to be an historian in the academic world—you must teach. In America, perhaps more than in Australia, you can be a writer and historian without having academic credentials. There are lots of what we call 'freedomists', in fact, perhaps the most successful American historian right now would be David McCullough and he doesn't have a PhD.

You don't always have a choice but when you do have a choice—I was offered a job at Johns Hopkins University and I was told that I didn't have to teach as much, or something like that—it would not be my dream to work in a library all the time doing research. However, some historians want that. They say, 'I am only teaching to make a living, but if I did what I wanted to do, I would be writing or researching all the time.'

CA Does it improve your writing to have student interaction and an audience on which to try things?

JACKSON You know, I think perhaps it does, because you are always talking to people who don't always have the context. So you are always thinking about how to make it make sense to them. I don't always do it well, but I always try to relate it to their experience. If you are going to teach, somehow you have to act like you care about where they are coming from.

That is not always easy if you are from some minor Caribbean country—I mean why should American history be important to you if you are from somewhere like this? But I still think you should attempt to make it relevant.

CA You have said that little history is being taught to youngsters. Do you think American history should be a compulsory subject at secondary school?

JACKSON I do think it should be compulsory because I think history is more important in the United States than it is in Denmark or Germany or Israel, or places where your citizenship is defined by your blood. I think where your citizenship is defined by a set of ideals, it really emerges from your history.

We don't have a religion, we don't have a race, we don't have common interests, all we have is a set of principles, which really emerge out of our history. Somebody was saying, 'How can you become a New Yorker in America?' Well, you just say you want to. You can't change your blood but you can change the set of ideas that you accept. Therefore, the Battle of Gettysburg could be important for somebody who only got here a couple of years ago. It was a battle fought 150 years ago but it was for principles and ideals that are every bit as relevant now as they were then.

CA You have stated that the way history is taught in secondary schools is boring. How can you make history more interesting for students?

JACKSON I think one of the problems we have now is that we are increasingly moving to testing facts in schools on the theory that this is better for the students. I am reluctant to say that. I think most people who take an interest in the past have been inspired by some teacher, or some person in their past. It doesn't even matter what that teacher was inspired by, it is just that they were so excited about something that they got me excited about it. And I think that when they teach to a test, which is to them just a list of dates and people they have to teach, that is a recipe for being bored.

You have to interest the students and then the facts will come later. I mean, if you put the facts first—let me think of an example, like the Kennedy assassination or even the conspiracy theory about the World Trade Center—if you ever talked to any of those people they would be full of facts. How wide the wings were, who heard the other explosions and what time? They are buried in facts but the first thing they got interested in was the question. It's the same with the Kennedy assassination. I don't mean to use them as an example. It's just that you have to have passion about it; be passionate about something, care about it. You have to find something in it that interests and speaks to you.

I heard Simon Schama talking about an eighth grade teacher in England who inspired him and made him love the past. This teacher 'grabbed' him and made him into a different kind of person. I hope that people love what they do because if you don't love what you do then you aren't going to inspire anyone.

CA What about the problem of hiring adjunct staff instead of tenure-track professors?

JACKSON That is part of the larger American problem of measuring everything by money and trying to make everything and everyone competitive with something or someone else. If Chase Manhattan Bank is not returning as much profit on its capital investment as Citibank, that means people have to be fired. The same happens now with the colleges, they are trying to attract the superstars—as Americans, we are very competitive with our colleges, even at the very top! They still want one hundred thousand people to apply so that they can turn down ninety-nine thousand! They want to build facilities to make them happy and they want to have star professors, meanwhile they have to cut someone else. The way they do it, in lots of places, is that they won't hire full-time, tenure-track people with benefits. It is much cheaper to hire people to teach one course for which you pay them not even barely a minimum wage—$5000 or so, to teach a whole course—and they have no rights, no job security, no long term commitment to the institution. However, if it helps the bottom line of the department or the college, then that is what they are doing. Right now there is no effective way to fight that. We have seen a rising number of adjuncts, a very sharp rise in the last quarter of a century.

CA I read that your *Crabgrass Frontier: The Suburbanization of the United States* has been reprinted twenty times and *The Encyclopedia of New York City* is in its sixth printing. Is it because you have a certain style that is appealing? What is it that makes your books so widely read?

JACKSON *Crabgrass* is up to twenty-five reprints now. First, I think, too often, historians only consider what is interesting to them. Second, too often, they want to rush it into print too fast and don't pay enough attention to their writing. Third, and most perniciously, there is a theory that a Professor of English at the University of California, Berkeley, summed up when he said that professors ought to be obscure because we really don't want the larger population to be part of the conversation. I think that it is arrogant to assume that anyone who is important or interesting or knowledgeable works inside the university. There are an awful lot of smart people, doing something else, who are interested in history. They are not required to read these books and so you have to appeal to them. You have to make things relevant.

Most professors are not in the business of torture. When you read feedback from students that a book is boring and not worth their time, most professors, unless for a special reason, will drop that book. I tried to write *Crabgrass Frontier* for an educated generalist—somebody who I assume is intelligent but has no interest in what I am doing. So it is my job to convince them that the question is important and that the answer to that could be interesting. You have to really work at it. I don't think good writing comes easily to anybody but a few geniuses, of which I obviously am not one, so you have to do the hard work. It's hard work. It's really hard, hard work. Even someone like Hemingway said that good writing was the result of good re-writing and he stood up all the time, but he was remembered! It is a hard job and anyone who doesn't think it is hard to write isn't a very good writer.

CA Do you use film and documentaries when you teach? I know you are in quite a few documentaries, yourself, especially on New York.

JACKSON I use some documentary films, but not as often as I am in them! I think the widest use of American documentary films is on television, one way or another. How often do they get used in classes? I really don't know. I do use them, myself, but I have been criticised for it. I do think that it is another obligation on us. It is a different group, it is a different medium and I don't think it is a waste of time [to show documentary films]. Where do people learn history? There is the National Park Service—the park rangers are where a lot of people get history from. Another place is museums, another is from documentary films and the worse place, is feature films.

I think history is exciting, I don't think you don't have to fake it. It always infuriates me when I see something like the *Gangs of New York* and they have war ships firing on the city. War ships didn't fire on the city in the 1863 riots and there was more than enough dramatic and tragic material to work with. You don't have to make up stuff; just go with what's there. Do you know how often in real life you say, 'You couldn't make that stuff up'? That's really true. And when you talk about history, you are talking about the most interesting parts of it. I think we should try to get it right and I think that we should communicate to students that we are trying to get it right.

In the United States, there is a great suspicion about the Left and Right concerning history. The conservatives' line—or let's say the Republicans' line—is that history has been shanghaied by a group of Leftist professors who are trying to convince us that the Japanese were mistreated when we dropped the atomic bomb on them, and the cold war was our fault, or something like that. And they believed that we've distorted it. On the Left, they say that history was written by and for rich people. No-one is very interested in the truth. So both sides think we are really propagandists of some sort.

I think that our job is to say, first of all: 'We love the past. We do think there is something in the past that is helpful for us to know, which perhaps helps us understand where we came from. We don't really have a personal stake in lying to everybody. We actually like the quest. If you can prove to us that we have been wrong somewhere then we will go after it.'

Basically we enjoy the topic, at least as much as proving our own point. We have a real tough task in the United States because there is real suspicion, and I'm not making this up—on both sides—that history is a fairytale. Nobody wants to know the real truth. Historians really do want to know the real truth. We have given our lives to do this and we are not making a lot of money, so what is in it for us to protect either side?

CA You teach a very famous course called The History of New York. Are your students mainly New Yorkers or international students?

JACKSON Because Columbia is an 'elite institution', it tries very hard to get a diverse student body. Most of the students, by definition, are not from New York. But I also feel that people who love New York the most, are not from New York. New Yorkers tend to take it for granted. But for those of us who were born in a different environment, we realise that there is something great about New York City. There is something magical about it and there is something precious about it, something that was threatened on 9/11. The city is a vulnerable thing, both in its physical form and its psychological form, and both can be destroyed. I would say that both are at risk and both can be lost, and by that I mean the city is a place of openness and toleration and excitement and vitality. If it becomes a police state … Berlin is one of the great cities in the world but I think in the 1930s it was not a great city. I think you can erode the greatness of a city just by making it too much of a place of order. I think that we are drifting in that direction at the moment in New York. We still have a long way to go before we will be on a par with Germany. Nonetheless, I think there is a definite move towards this with all the new ways of tracking cell phones, tracking easy pass, Metro cards to ATMs to cameras everywhere, to tracking credit cards, tracking everything about your telephones, social security numbers. The power of the state or the government and the police to regulate life has been ratcheted up enormously in the last twenty-five years and I hope that we don't ever let the scale tip too far. If you really want perfect safety or perfect graciousness, go to a small town. If you want to roll the dice and say, 'I don't know what tomorrow will bring', then come to the big cities.

CA If you were in another city and you were doing a history of that city, would it work as well, or is it just the magic of New York?

JACKSON You can kind of generalise about suburbs and you can also generalise about cities, but I think that in Australia or in the United States that most cities are unique places and if you spent time, you could look at an area, photograph it and say, 'Well, that's Melbourne, not Adelaide, not Perth. Or that's Cincinnati, not Chicago, not St Louis.' They are different and they have unique personalities, almost like people do. So in that sense, I do think New York is the greatest of American cities, indeed I think it is the greatest of all cities, but just like I think Abraham Lincoln was a great president, it doesn't mean you only write biographies of him. And I think cities are interesting. I think our challenge now is that we have not been writing what I would call accessible urban history, so it is very much out of fashion right now to write an urban biography of the United States. There was a time when we did that, I think there will be another time. It is certainly not true now.

CA Do you think if 9/11 had happened somewhere else, like Los Angeles instead of New York, that there would have been a different reaction, because the community spirit in New York binds people together?

JACKSON That's a hard one. I don't know if I would go out on a limb and say that New Yorkers would be any better than others. I do think it [the response to 9/11] was one of New York's best moments. I think Giuliani handled himself pretty well but more than that I think the citizens as a whole were running downtown and trying to do what they could—not abandoning the subways and not abandoning the city, which was what a lot of people thought. And the way you could tell they didn't was from real estate prices—real estate prices going down would mean people wanted to leave—but they were going up. So, I think, at least locally there is a little more kindness amongst people. I don't want to push that too hard but I am not the only person who has said that.

I don't think it would have had the dramatic impact if it had happened in some other city, I think the terrorists knew that. I think if you bombed the French Quarter in New Orleans it would have been sad—I think it would have been a huge story—but I think the collapse of the World Trade Center was something else. This is because those buildings were symbolic around the world and nobody had ever seen a collapse of that magnitude—it was a collapse that would capture your attention in Istanbul or Tokyo in a way that it wouldn't have if it was a bomb that went off. You could see it; you could see it live. By the time you have heard about a bombing, it is already over, so all you are looking at is debris. The way the World Trade Center played out was almost like the four acts of a play and so, increasingly, people were there. The first impact was seen by bystanders, the second time, millions of people were watching and then when the buildings came down, the whole world was watching. I do think the impact was greater, plus, you wouldn't have had all those fire fighters or responders dying in some other kind of tragedy, I don't think. I think sacrificing the fire fighters made some kind of difference. That's a controversial thing, and I argued with a guy the other day who said that it was a total waste of lives and that we hadn't come to terms with the fact that the fire fighters were on a suicide mission—it was a mistake to send them up there. Now obviously, in retrospect, it was a mistake but I do think at the time that they performed a service of calming people and since that time there has been a psychological benefit.

CA Has the car destroyed the sense of community?

JACKSON I sort of think so. It hasn't destroyed it but it has very much eroded the sense of community where people used to walk and pass people on their front porches and on the sidewalk; went to the local school because they could ride their bike or walk there; went to the local butcher shop, the local delicatessen and the local shoe repair. I think that is different from getting in a car and going to a gigantic big box retailer where everyone has to pay hourly employees; where you have to get there by car; where you go across the car park at certain prescribed hours that is private property; where you couldn't hand out a leaflet. I think that is very different from the shared space of a city. A shopping mall is a private space and protest—disagreement—is not allowed on private space. And I don't think Americans have realised what they have lost.

'The life of the imagination goes on everywhere' *Stephen Greenblatt*

All heads turn when Greenblatt enters the room. He has just returned from Japan. In fact, we were probably in Japan at the same time. But I had the obligatory stopover with Northwest airlines in order to save $500.00 and Greenblatt has just viewed the premiere of a version of his play in the East. His walk is the walk of a man who is self-assured, confident about his importance and prepossessed. And why shouldn't he be? A quick google of 'Greenblatt, Stephen' reveals that he is a 'brilliant scholar', 'world renowned scholar of renaissance literature', 'eminent scholar and critic'. Greenblatt is the golden boy of academe. Dubbed 'The Father of New Historicism', he looks far younger than you would imagine. But then he has had a fortunate life. Poached by Harvard from Berkeley, Greenblatt's title is officially the 'Harry Levin Professor of Literature' and he has the luxury of flying all over the world as a visiting professor and scholar.

I first saw the name 'Greenblatt' on the cover of my Norton Anthology of English Literature, but it was with the publication of Hamlet in Purgatory *(2001) and* Will in the World *(2004) that I understood that he was setting himself up as a Shakespearean expert, among other things. He lists his interests as Shakespeare; Early Modern Literature and Culture; Literature of Travel and Exploration; Religion and Literature; Literature and Anthropology; Literary and Cultural Theory and so I was more than a little intimidated when, being granted an interview, I found myself on a polished wooden chair outside his office door at Harvard.*

Greenblatt seems to have a lot of people working for him. There is a busy feeling in the big open plan office. When he arrives, a flock of administrative staff greet Greenblatt and ask him about his trip and his family. He is in no rush and answers their questions in detail before leading me into his office. By contrast, it is incredibly small. He sits behind his desk and I perch on the chair opposite him. There is something easy-going about his demeanour and coupled with his blue jeans and casual top he appears quite affable, but I'm not really that sure that I even rate a blip on his radar. He kicks back nonchalantly putting his feet up on the desk as he continuously throws an eraser in the air. Greenblatt likes to perform, and so it is no wonder that his lectures are packed with students.

He stops tossing the eraser in the air and leans back on his chair with his hands behind his head. His feet are still crossed on the desk and I wonder if he will fall, but he has it all under control. Greenblatt is exactly where he wants to be. He has all the will in the world to succeed.

CA I am particularly interested in the way that writing informs teaching and perhaps even the less discussed notion of teaching informing writing. You have stated: 'My students have had a profound intelligence upon everything I have written.' How do writing and teaching influence one another? Is the connection between you and your students a two-way process?

GREENBLATT Yes, of course. It's a two-way process, not only because of the questions the students have and the input that they have, which is considerable, but because the whole idea of a sharp differentiation between the two is artificial. What does one write for? I mean one writes to communicate with people whom one hopes are interested, and if you can't, as a teacher, start with your students, then it's not quite clear with whom you are trying to communicate.

CA Is it important for literary critics to work in the academy? There is a lot of discussion that it would be better not to and Dana Gioia has talked about this with reference to poetry. He said that academics end up being 'gatekeepers of the canon' when you work in a university. Do you feel you have a responsibility for what your students read, what you introduce them to—those sorts of things?

GREENBLATT I obviously have some relation to what they read not only in my courses but also in general as part of the curriculum. I take this seriously and in multiple senses; one of the hats that I wear is as the general editor of the *Norton Anthology of English Literature* and that is, for better or worse, one of the ways in which the idea of the canon is formed at this point in the late twentieth/early twenty-first century, so of course I think of that. On the whole, however, I have to confess that I think of my enterprise more in the language of pleasure than I do in the language of obligation. I do feel the weight of pedagogical responsibility, but the responsibility has to start with one's sense of what constitutes a deep and gratifying reading experience for oneself.

I actually learnt this in my very first year of teaching at Berkeley many years ago. I assigned something I didn't like and then I hated teaching it; I hated the whole experience. I realised I should never do that again; I should only teach what is already giving me pleasure, what I feel I should grapple with myself. Having said that, I am teaching a course in the fall with a wonderful colleague of mine, Louis Menand, that is essentially a quest for the set of books that we feel all undergraduates should read before they graduate from college. But the 'should read' is not about moral obligation but rather is a part of what is exciting about being a human being, being a late adolescent.

CA Over the course of a year, how is your time divided between writing and teaching?

GREENBLATT I certainly take a break, but I don't sharply differentiate between the time I am teaching and the time that I am writing, partly because in the time that I am writing and not teaching I often have graduate students or lots of things that are pedagogical. But then when I am teaching, I try and make time to write. Academics at Harvard have, roughly speaking, fairly light teaching loads and relatively light numbers of hours in the classroom, so all the hours they are not in the classroom are spent in classroom-related activities. However, much of this involves writing and the writing feeds into the teaching and the teaching feeds into the writing.

CA There is some debate about creative writing in universities in Australia, specifically at the PhD level. Should there be a PhD in creative writing with no theoretical component?

GREENBLATT Off the top of my head, without thinking about it very much, I would have been slightly sceptical as to whether to be in the PhD program is the best way of developing one's skills as a writer. On the other hand, to develop one's curriculum vitae so that one can get a job, if that's what it takes, I can see why there's a strong link there. There are people in this department, creative artists, who have PhDs but they have PhDs in literature. You should talk to them about whether they think it's a good idea, they have a strong sense of what it should be. I certainly have plenty of undergraduates who do creative writing theses. I have graduate students who are poets or fiction writers in addition to being academic writers. My relationship to my students is mostly about training people to do scholarly work. I wouldn't feel comfortable about teaching someone doing a purely creative writing thesis—I wouldn't know how to grade it, I wouldn't know how to teach it—but there are people in this department who probably would.

CA How do you teach Shakespeare at university? Do you encourage it to be read aloud or study key passages?

GREENBLATT There are lots of different ways; there is not a single way of doing it. I suppose I would have to say that my default mode is not anything fancy at all except that we talk about writers, pick out different scenes in the play and look hard at them to try and see what is going on moment to moment. I sometimes show films or talk about what's going on in the scenes. Because I am a ham, I like to ham it up and read things dramatically or show what alternative readings can be applied to lines in a play.

Also, in the last couple of years I taught a course called Shakespearean Playwriting in which the students try to write scenes from lost Shakespeare plays or try to figure out what he does and try to imitate it and play with imitating it. So that would be another way of trying to get people to see that, of course, Shakespeare is an extraordinary genius but also that he has a set of skills—students can figure out what that skill set is, what the choices that he is making are, what he likes and what he doesn't like to do. This is one of the ways of doing an assignment.

CA I have read that students have abandoned other courses to choose your course because of your readings and teaching methods. How are you an inspiring teacher?

GREENBLATT I love teaching but I think it is quite hard to teach. I enjoy it and I know very well that there are people who have extraordinary and genuine vocations as teachers, magical vocations—when you see it, you know what it is. I think I am okay at taking my responsibility seriously and taking pleasure in it, but I don't take myself, to be honest with you Cassandra, as having some kind of fantastic vocation.

When I was an undergraduate, one of my teachers was Vincent Scully, an art historian who was just amazing, I couldn't quite believe what he was quite doing—he was so passionate and dramatic and it poured out of him as if it was effortless for him to speak that way. I love it when I see it but I don't think I have that gift.

CA I have read about your first experience reading *As You Like It* at high school and you said, 'Though I have spent much of my adult life thinking about Shakespeare, my first encounter with Shakespeare was a disaster. In junior high school I found *As You Like It* quite possibly the most tedious and annoying thing I had ever read.'

GREENBLATT It was junior high school. That makes a difference. I must have been thirteen or fourteen and I was too young. It was a very sophisticated play. It is always hard to understand the choices that people make for teaching small children Shakespeare. But *As You Like It*—which I think is a marvellous play—struck me as a very dodgy choice.

CA How do you recommend that you instil a love of Shakespeare in high school students so they are not soured by the experience?

GREENBLATT Having just said that, I would add that if a teacher is powerful enough, almost anything—even the phone book—can come across as an ineffable thing. It would be very hard for me to say there was a rule for it, except that being passionately in love with the subject seems to me to help; if you actually care about the thing. Looking back on my *As You Like It* class, I just can't imagine that Miss Gillespie, or whatever her name was, cared about this play at all since it was a dull class.

But a few years later I had a crack at *King Lear*, which certainly must be a harder play to teach than *As You Like It*, but I found it incredibly thrilling. The teacher had a tremendous gift and he engaged in a vigorous and brooding way which remains with me now, some forty five years later, as a vision of what it is to actually communicate to people—why it matters, why caring about the play actually matters. What I remember from that particular experience, which was with a teacher named John Harris who is dead now, was that he was quite humble in relation to the text. There were moments in which he couldn't understand what was happening and admitted to us that he didn't quite actually know what was going on; didn't pretend that he knew.

When I was at school, the thing that I found most depressing was the air of the teacher who knew absolutely everything—there was no struggle involved and it was all somehow recollected in tranquility. I like people who are actually wrestling with learning a little bit more.

CA You have said, 'The idea that you need an advanced degree to understand Shakespeare is a joke'? Why do you think Shakespeare's works are considered by people to be so difficult? Do you think reading is in decline? Are people unwilling to struggle with a text anymore?

GREENBLATT Well, I don't know why I said that Shakespeare isn't difficult. Of course, in some ways he is difficult because the stuff was written a long time ago in 1600. By the time you reach 2000, the language has changed, and his rhetoric is very dense and complicated. What I meant when I said that, I suppose, is that what is amazing about Shakespeare is that he can, even after such a long time, be graspable by an enormously wide range of people—so that elementary school children and high school girls and so forth can watch and understand. But it does usually involve watching and performing the play more than reading.

Reading Shakespeare is hard for anyone, so I think the first thing to say with Shakespeare is that his plays were written to be performed. Simply teaching Shakespeare—and this is the way I was taught—by giving the text to someone who is fifteen or sixteen-years old and saying 'read', is a little bit like opening a score to *Cosi Fan Tutte* and saying, 'now enjoy Mozart'. You could reach a point in which you could open the score and take tremendous pleasure in it, but it's easier if you have actually heard

Cosi Fan Tutte first. In most of Shakespeare's plays there is an enormous range, or at least in the great plays, there are a range of things you can see. If I were teaching in high school I would certainly make heavy use of the fact that you can watch these things being performed. *Romeo and Juliet* can be difficult but once you've seen Kate Winslet [sic. Claire Danes] or whoever it was, Leonardo DiCaprio, there is so much going on, you don't get the whole of it, but you do get something of it.

CA You have stated that although the relationship in *Shakespeare in Love* is implausible, that it is an entertaining film nonetheless. What do you think of modern adaptations of Shakespeare?

GREENBLATT On adaptations and modernisations and transformations of the plays, I'm not actually someone who feels that it is very important to leave the plays alone and not do things with them. The way and spirit in which Shakespeare's plays are written involves manhandling. The plays were written to be transformed—that doesn't mean we should forget about the scripts that we have from four hundred years ago—but I think that it is fair game to do anything you want with them. They can be a disaster as well. In film, in particular, often what happens is that one loses a lot of the play in order to substitute a kind of visual experience that will somehow convey what needs to be conveyed. You can't possibly fill it with all the words. One should probably not fight too strongly against that but accept that as the nature of the medium.

On the other hand, I don't know if this is your experience but I have often gone to weddings and some funerals in which people try to make up their own services. And sometimes it's marvellous but actually a lot of the time they would have been better off sticking with the book of common prayer, as it is very beautiful. So it is a risky undertaking if you discard a huge amount of Shakespeare and just make it up yourself. You can succeed brilliantly but you can also fail terribly.

CA You have discussed in interviews the importance of both reading and performance, not just one at the expense of the other.

Is it hard after spending a lifetime thinking about Shakespeare to stay in touch with the wonder?

GREENBLATT Something that is implicit in your question seems to me to be inherently true, and that if you've taught the same thing eight thousand times it gets rather more difficult to feel the full force of it, as if you were reading it for the first time. You can pretend that you do and every once in a while the pretense itself can be rather regenerating, but it is definitely harder to keep the freshness, and I don't pretend that it is not.

On the other hand, there is a huge amount of Shakespeare, and even though I have worked for years in this field, it turns out that there are all kinds of things that completely take me by surprise. Often this happens in performance. I always have this experience, that even in a mediocre performance of a play—and God knows I have seen many—I see something that I didn't see before; something in the intonation. It's not just the actor's cleverness, it is that suddenly you see that what looked like a familiar rock has been broken open and there is a crystal inside, that you didn't know was there. That is a way of recovering or regenerating things that you thought you knew too well. You get to know certain things very, very well so that they can be resonant for you. In the sense of taking your breath away, this experience diminishes. But then you can often recover it in the performance.

CA You have been dubbed the father of New Historicism and I was interested in your discussion of doing your work 'through techniques of association, analogy, surprising connection, things contingently leaning against each other, collage'. Why do you think that criticism has moved from textual to contextual interpretation?

GREENBLATT Well, I'm not sure it has, but in many cases, contextual work is 'in play' now. There are a number of different explanations, one of which is the growing resistance to the assumption, implicit in traditional close reading, that there is a single group of specialists who control the life of the imagination, and who are considered to be its masters. That is, textual interpretation tended to wall off the works of artists deemed worthy of serious attention from all other forms of expression and to imply that no one else could even begin to play the game, let alone justify sustained analysis. I think that this impulse to isolate has given way to something else. Contextual interpretation does not abandon the recognition of genius, but it understands that any artistic game, that's well played, is almost always enormously wide-spread, not only in works of art but also in lots of other life experience—that is why it actually reaches people.

So the first step and finally the last step for any contextual work is to understand that the imagination is not walled off in the special objects we call literature, but the life of the imagination goes on everywhere. The question is how to tap into that and how to share the life of the imagination, put it in contact with these objects. A contextual work's success or power has to do with the democratisation of the idea of the imagination and feeling that it is not only a handful of artists and their professorial expositors who control this thing—it is not actually under anyone's control, it is there in the collective life of our societies. I love that feeling. Actually, sometimes it's scary—after all, literature is full of accounts of terror and hatred as well as joy and love. But the truth of the matter is that people live lives that are not driven solely by rational calculation but by extraordinary, very strange acts of the imagination. Literary objects are uniquely in touch with those, but they are in touch with those precisely because they are spread so widely.

CA Who do you admire among Shakespeare scholars?

GREENBLATT Huge numbers. There are a million people who are doing wonderful work on Shakespeare. If we are talking not only of specialist works but also of books that reach a broader public, I just read with great pleasure Jim Shapiro's book called *A Year In The Life of William Shakespeare*. My colleague, Marge Garber, has written a book that is addressed to a fairly broad public about all of the plays. My former teacher, Harold Bloom, has certainly managed to reach a very broad reading public. Then within the world of the academy there are unending numbers of people doing wonderful things on more specialised work. I greatly admire

Margreta de Grazia at the University of Pennsylvania; Julia Lupton, a relatively young person at the University of California, published a remarkable book recently on citizenship and Shakespeare; Paul Kottman, a still younger theorist and scholar at the New School in New York; and the list goes on.

CA *Will in the World* illustrates the historical context of Shakespeare's life and work. Were you surprised by the reaction to the book?

GREENBLATT I was delighted of course. I hoped it was going to be a success, but the fact that it reached a very, very broad public and was well received made me enormously happy, and it did surprise me. It surprised me a little bit for the same reason that the success of the movie *Shakespeare In Love* surprised me—what was amazing to me about *Shakespeare In Love* was that millions of people became involved in what was fundamentally a literary question: how is it possible for this person to go from being the author of *Two Gentlemen of Verona* to being the author of *Romeo and Juliet*? The movie's answer was a creative one: Gwyneth Paltrow. But behind Gwyneth Paltrow is the sense that there must have been something in his life as well as his talent that enabled him to do what he did. In effect, that is what *Will in the World* articulated as well, that there's something about the way he was in his world, about his interactions, about how that world was in addition to the native genius that he had, that must help us to understand what he did.

Sometimes Harold Bloom gets on a very high horse about these responses and about me. I don't have any problem with Harold Bloom—he was my teacher, I respect and admire him—and I have no problem with the quasi-hierophantic, theological feelings that he generates towards Shakespeare, as he rolls his eyes up and says 'This was God; this was a great genius.' Shakespeare *was* an astonishing genius, that seems true, even a truism, but the question is, what is the relationship between that genius and the world he was living in? What kind of life was he living? Who did he love? Who did he hate? Who was he afraid of? Who amused him? What did he care about? How did he get a sense of his vocation? How did he do what he did? So that was the set of questions that very much provoked me and I was delighted that it worked in its form because the general reading public has a largely untapped passionate interest in literature but a deep resistance towards what we normally write as literary criticism. This kind of work is generally not read at all, except by people forced to, by assigning it to them. And that is crazy. It is crazy on our part since we should actually figure out a way of addressing the genuine interest that people have. It is not an academic interest, it's not because they have been assigned it, but because they care about it.

CA I think it can sometimes become too jargonistic and for the average person to read mystifying prose about Shakespeare, depending on what school of literary criticism you are writing from, that can be very difficult.

GREENBLATT The mistake is to think that you have to sacrifice your intelligence to write clearly because you can actually write very complex things in clear prose. The world is full of people who have done it. This tradition starts with Shakespeare's own achievement, but extends to many other people.

CA Can you talk about the play you wrote and what you were doing with it in Japan?

GREENBLATT It was fascinating. With a playwright named Charles Mee, I wrote a play called *Cardenio* based on Shakespeare's lost play, but ours is set in the twenty-first century. I look forward to seeing the English language premiere in the United States this spring, but this was not my only interest in the project. Because my concern is cultural mobility, I contacted a range of theatre companies in different places and made a proposal to them. I said our play could not be directly translated but that it could be adapted and transformed. My goal was to see what happened when it moved from one culture to another. I saw a production in Japan by a wonderful playwright called Akio Miyazawa and a production in Bengali in Calcutta, with ones coming up in Croatian in Zagreb and in Spanish in Madrid. It seems to me fascinating to see what happens when it moves around from one place to another. [*He holds up the Japanese poster.*] They called it *Motorcycle Don Quixote* (not my idea but I can't complain because I got into it for precisely this purpose—to see what would happen to it when it got moved around from one place to another). It was fascinating; it was very, very deeply interesting to see this piece. I engaged in this whole project partly to get at what I take to be Shakespeare's own practice and also what's happened to Shakespeare. That is to say, his own practice very much involves taking things and transforming them, making them other than they were, borrowing from them but also making them no longer resemble what they were when he began. I wanted to set up a kind of experimental space in which I could watch this process of metamorphosis happen with the text that Charles Mee and I wrote, and that's what has happened.

'Tradition is a romance'
Dana Gioia

Chairman Gioia is charismatic. Boyishly handsome, exceedingly intelligent, powerful and yet somehow humble. I read his groundbreaking article, 'Can Poetry Matter?' before I read any of his poetry and I found myself nodding at the end of every line. He is honest. Refreshingly honest. And instead of just mourning the state of poetry, he has ideas for a better future. Chairman Gioia looks for a way forward. But most importantly he makes things happen. I am still fascinated by the Big Read Project (details below) and the way he manages not only to be Chairman for the National Endowment of the Arts, but poet, critic, librettist, anthologist, translator, man of letters and, of course, family man.

When I found Gioia's impressive website (www.danagioia.net), I spent all afternoon entranced, reading his biography, his poetry and criticism. At that time I had no idea he was the Chairman. Gioia's credentials are impressive. He is winner of the American Book Award and his poems, translations, essays and reviews have appeared in magazines such as The New Yorker, The Atlantic, The Washington Post Book World, The New York Times Book Review, Slate *and* The Hudson Review. *He has published three books of poetry:* Daily Horoscope *(1986),* The Gods of Winter *(1991) and* Interrogations at Noon (2001). *He has translated poetry from Latin, Italian, German and Romanian. His critical works include the incredible* Can Poetry Matter? Essays on Poetry and American Culture *(1992),* Barrier of a Common Language: An American Looks at Contemporary British Poetry *(2003) and he has written the libretto for* Nosferatu, *an opera.*

I was planning to travel to Washington D.C. in July and so I emailed Gioia to ask if I could interview him. His personal assistant answered me the next day and I was granted a half hour interview with the Chairman in his office. With everyone referring to him as 'The Chairman', I was very nervous about meeting him. I arrived early at 1100 Pennsylvania Ave. I was an hour early—I am always early for interviews. But this time I didn't sit outside and wait. The Chairman's office is above a shopping centre!

There is a lot of security and once you get passed security there are personal assistants to meet before you get into Gioia's office. One of his personal assistants remained for the duration of the interview. But when he walked up to me, shook my hand, looked me right in the eye and said, 'Hello I'm Dana, pleased to meet you', my concerns melted away at the sound of his mellifluous voice. The chairman made me feel right at home. We sat at the table in his huge office. But it was more like a room or a study in someone's house than somewhere corporate. I started my tape recorder and initially it wouldn't work. But even then the Chairman was charming and told me that 'Gioia' means 'joy' in Italian. And then the little wheels of the recorder started turning again.

CA Would you say that you are living proof the American Dream is still alive and well? Your life has been summed up as the working-class kid who carved a career in the arts.

GIOIA Perhaps, but if so, I am only one of millions of Americans who have created their own lives. One of the advantages of the United States is a considerable freedom to shape your own future. My own bizarre life has been fashioned and re-fashioned several times across the years.

CA You give so much of yourself and your personal life in your work. Why do you feel it is important to share these experiences with your audience?

GIOIA I find most public speeches boring. When I talk to an audience, I try above all else not to be dull and dopey. I've learned that sometimes the best way to communicate with an audience is to tell stories from your own life. If you are a public figure, you also have a certain obligation to introduce yourself to the public. I am by nature a very intellectual person. When I was younger, I spoke mostly in ideas. Now I try to start from my own experience and only gradually introduce some general ideas. The personal becomes the foundation for the intellectual.

CA Is it hard, though, when you have to talk about something intensely personal, especially something that might have been difficult for you to overcome?

GIOIA Yes, it was hard at first. If you talk about your life, you have to include the blunders, defeats, and sorrows. When I first tried this approach, I was awkward because I didn't want to seem self-indulgent or self-promoting. I am a reserved person. I don't usually blurt out intimate details of my life. But a friend of mine recommended that I take a more personal approach. She was right. I was able to reach the audience more effectively. Maybe it's something women know better than men—that you communicate best by creating an emotional link with the listener.

CA In 2001 you founded 'Teaching Poetry'. How do you improve high school teaching of poetry?

GIOIA I was asked by some people in California to create a new writers' conference. They said I could focus on any topic that interested me. I was actually rather bewildered by this freedom. I thought about it for months. Then it occurred to me that the most underserved group in literary culture were high school teachers. These people taught kids at a pivotal moment in their lives—adolescence—when teenagers create their adult identities. These teachers helped determine whether the new generation would be readers or not. They were especially important to creating a future generation of poetry readers.

CA Why was there not such a conference already in existence?

GIOIA It offered no professional advantages to the power-brokers of literary culture. If you're a professor at a research university, you don't get promoted by helping high school teachers. The most influential people in literary America pretty much ignored the high school experience because there is no prestige in serving it. It struck me that if I wanted to improve American literary culture, high school was the place where there was both the greatest need and the greatest opportunity. If you can encourage and sustain readers at fifteen or sixteen, they may read for the rest of their lives.

CA You support the canonical literary tradition. Had this had widespread support?

GIOIA I'm not sure what it means to support the canonical literary tradition because the canon changes every year. There are books that now seem absolutely central to the literary canon that nobody read fifty years ago. When T. S. Eliot wrote 'Tradition and the Individual Talent' ninety years ago, he was the first to notice that every time a major new work of art comes along, it changes our whole conception of the past.

CA What do you believe in then?

GIOIA I believe in something different from a fixed canonical past. I believe that for the present to understand itself, it has to refer to the past. The present looks at the past to see how it can create a better future. I don't know any way of creating new art without considering what art has or hasn't done in the past. There are dozens of traditions. The canon is vast and fluid. If you are only reading books written in the last ten years, then you have a certain myopia about art.

American culture is obsessed with novelty. You see this in nowhere more obviously than in television, which is always trying to sell you something new. Serious art differs from consumer entertainment because it has broader affinities that go all the way back to the past and bring more of the world into each work. In that sense, I am a traditionalist. I don't see any way of being a real artist without loving tradition. Tradition isn't an intimidating marble temple. It is a romance that enlivens and enlarges your life.

CA You have said that when you were at university, 'I wasn't being trained to be a writer. I was being trained to be a professor.' Do you think that a university education is sometimes inimical to writing? So should, or can, universities teach writing, especially creative writing?

GIOIA I am not anti-academic. The university remains the scholarly centre of culture. The problem is that today the university often assumes it possesses a monopoly on literary culture. That seems ridiculously parochial. Literary culture is broad and diverse. It includes publishing, journalism, broadcast, and bohemia as well as academia. If you want to learn to write well, you may be better off nowadays working in journalism than getting an academic degree. At least journalists have remained professional communicators in a way that academics have not. But, of course, journalism has its own dangers for a young writer. The best possible background for a writer is probably a diverse one that combines serious academic study with the daily engagement and public responsibility of journalism. Anyone who wants to be a writer nowadays should go to the university but then get out of it.

CA I read in an interview posted on your website how you came to write the libretto for *Nosferatu*. You also describe how the film brings back memories of your childhood. I wanted to ask you about your ability to capture the sensuality of the Dracula myth and our fear of mortality, which you have described as being the basic existential dilemma from which genuine poetry grows. What was it like working with these themes? Was it difficult to write something that would be equally interesting on the page as on the stage?

GIOIA Writing an opera libretto is a curious challenge for a poet. Poets are used to composing small works for the page, but drama opens up a certain power and resonance that is unique to the stage. You not only tell stories, you embody them in dramatic action. Working with a composer, you can also wrap all the power of music and song around those actions. I found writing a libretto a difficult but intoxicating undertaking. There are certain truths that you can only communicate as stories. There are certain mental and emotional states that you can communicate most clearly in performance. You feel the particular power of the operatic form when you see the work performed on stage.

One of the advantages the librettist has today is the technology of supertitles. The audience can see every line of the text. Both times that *Nosferatu* was produced, the company used supertitles. I could tell how effective that was. Afterwards an instructively large number of people told me they had had an unexpected literary experience while watching the opera. To their surprise, they experienced the opera as poetic drama. The operatic stage is the last portion of the theatre world in which the poet is a necessary collaborator.

CA Did anything surprise you in writing your libretto?

GIOIA The final libretto in *Nosferatu* contained many themes that I had never dealt with before in my poetry or I had only dealt with tangentially. This was especially true of the very dark material—especially the dangerous side of sexuality, and the death wish. Over the years I have noticed the power of the death wish—the longing for the peace of oblivion. People do things that they know are destructive, but they become intoxicated by the thrill of danger—drugs, drinking, violence, sex. It's a powerful subject matter that I had never really gotten into apart from a few poems. By using the vampire myth, *Nosferatu* allowed me to explore these themes in a way which surprised me once I was finished.

CA Do readers become writers? I know your reading as a child was nurtured by you inheriting your uncle's library. How important is an early reading role model or mentor?

GIOIA It is impossible to become a writer without first being a reader. Passionate reading is the precondition to literary creation. You fall in love with the medium. You drink it. You breathe it. You dream it. And eventually, you become it. Reading awakens our imagination. It develops our inner life. It refines our powers of articulation. I can tell right away when a young writer hasn't read enough: the language is stale, the ideas are clichéd, the standards are low.

CA Why did you begin your national campaign in 2005 to promote reading with the Big Read programme? How successful has it been? Why is it important for people to read good literature?

GIOIA The Big Read emerged out of a study the National Endowment for the Arts had done on American arts participation. We conducted what is probably the largest study of its kind in the world—which measured Americans' participation in all of the arts, including theatre, dance, music, museum-going, and reading. The study showed us a dramatic and universal decline in literary reading in the United States. Every group of Americans was reading less than they had ten years ago (and dramatically less than they did twenty years ago). There were declines in every group, regardless of age, gender, income, education, ethnicity, or region. The biggest decline was among younger adults who, in twenty years, had gone from the people who read the most in America to the ones who read the least.

CA Why was this decline important for anyone who wasn't a teacher or writer?

GIOIA I felt that there was a crisis, not simply in reading, but in American culture. Our data enabled us to correlate behaviour across all of the arts and civic involvement. We saw that people who read were two to three times more likely to do volunteer or charity work, to go to the theatre, to attend concerts, to visit museums. Readers were even twice as likely to go to sporting events. We observed that people who read were more involved in their communities and more involved in the arts. There is a phenomenon in ecological studies where a particular group, such as amphibians, can be used to indicate the overall health of the ecosystem. I think the key indicator for a democracy is reading. If you have universal literacy and active adult reading, then most other things in a democracy will be healthy. When you don't, you tend to develop a passive, alienated population.

CA But how did this cultural diagnosis result in the Big Read?

GIOIA Because of this study the NEA decided to create one national programme of ambition and effectiveness. The best thing I can say about the Big Read is that we did not invent the basic idea. We only improved on a grassroots one, which had been tried in a number of American communities to get people reading together. Most communities who had tried the idea liked it, but they didn't have the resources or skills to be able to repeat it or do it broadly. The Big Read is not about kids reading, it's about everybody reading. A community chooses a book, and the NEA develops television programming, radio programming, print programming, and educational materials to support that book, in addition to a grant that allows them to galvanize themselves.

CA How broadly have you tried the Big Read?

GIOIA We piloted it in ten American cities, ranging from a town of eleven hundred people to a metropolis of four million. Now we are expanding it into 200 cities across all 50 states. We've seen that you can get hundreds of organizations and institutions within a single community to partner up and reach every corner of the community. Ideally, we have every high school, every library branch, all the major cultural institutions, the newspaper, the leading radio station, television station, the chamber of commerce, and even retirement homes partnering with us to provide perhaps one hundred different events around the book. Fundamentally, serious literature becomes an on-going discussion in a community. A town can define its own character through reading. I think that's a very powerful civic notion.

CA You said once, 'I write more for my old fellow workers, who would never read my poems, than for the literati.' Is this still true? If so, does it encapsulate a lifelong tension for you between your background in working-class Los Angeles and your role today with the NEA?

GIOIA Absolutely. The dilemma of the modern poet is that you need to write for a general reader, but your gatekeepers are hyper-intellectual literati who are often out of touch with what a general reader wants. I write for an alert and intelligent non-specialist audience. I write for the common reader. Some people, especially academics, misunderstand that ambition. When I say 'common reader', I don't mean the common non-reader. I don't mean someone completely oblivious of art and ideas. What I'm talking about is probably half the population—intelligent, alert, curious people who probably have been so traumatized or so bored by studying poetry in school that they never want to read another poem.

CA But will these people listen to a poet?

GIOIA It has been my experience that if you can bring these people in touch with genuine poetry, they are the best audiences imaginable. If art is an enterprise which is only about artists talking to one another, then it is a very small thing. Literature is one of the great human expressions. It has the potential of reaching broad and mixed audiences. Literature is one of the ways that people stay in touch with their own humanity. So that is the paradoxical situation of the modern poet: You write for the reader who is convinced that he or she won't like your work.

CA Do you read any poets from Australia or New Zealand?

GIOIA Yes, I do. Unfortunately, very few poets from either country are widely read in the U.S., but back in my twenties I discovered A. D. Hope—quite by accident—and fell in love with his work. I suspect I like him more than Australians do. Then I began reading Judith Wright, James McAuley, Les Murray, Martin Johnson, Peter Porter, and John Tranter—an extremely fine line-up of poets. And, of course, I adore the amusing and fictive Ern Malley. I came to New Zealand poets a little later—mostly through James K. Baxter and Fleur Adcock. I am sure I've missed many fine poets because no-one in North America seems to champion your writers.

Your composers are also neglected. Peggy Glanville-Hicks is an astonishingly fine composer. Has there ever been a finer woman composer *anywhere*? Her operas in particular are major works. Yet in the U.S., where she lived for some years, she remains unknown. The New Zealand symphonist Douglas Lilburn also remains a well-known secret.

CA Just finally, I want to ask you about the future of poetry.

GIOIA The future of poetry is very bright, but it will probably be very different from the future that poetry professionals imagine. Let me give you one tiny instance. Poetry professionals tend to measure the success of poetry by the sales of books. A book of poems is not the best measure of poetry. The unit of cultural currency for poetry is the individual poem. Not only is the individual poem what people remember, but it is also a complete and free-standing work of art—like a painting or song. One nice thing about the individual poem is that it can be read on the radio or television. It can be recited in public. It can be downloaded off the internet as text or audio. It can reach millions who don't encounter it in a printed book.

The future of poetry, like most of the past of poetry, is going to be increasingly oral and performative. The electronic media has the power to reach more people than could easily have been done though print. That means poets will probably write a little differently. In America we have seen poetry regain a popular audience—largely because it's gone back to being off the page, which is where poetry began. Poetry is human speech raised to its highest levels of expressivity, concision, and memorability. That was the past of poetry, and I think it will also be the future of the art.

'Poetry Descends from the Sacred' *Camille Paglia*

I should admit that I have a bit of a girl crush on Camille Paglia. Her Sexual Personae: Art and Decadence from Nefertiti to Emily Dickinson *(1990) dominated my high school years. It was the best book of criticism I had ever read, and twenty-two years later, it stands the test of time. Her essay on Dickinson, in particular, is brilliant and I still assign it to my poetry students.* Sexual Personae *was followed by* Sex, Art, and American Culture *(1992);* Vamps and Tramps: New Essays *(1994), and her study of Alfred Hitchcock's* The Birds *(1998) published by the British Film Institute in its Film Classics Series. Seven years later, her fifth book,* Break, Blow, Burn: Camille Paglia Reads Forty-Three of the World's Best Poems, *was published. A national bestseller*, Break, Blow, Burn *is an extraordinary reading of selected poems. This collection of essays not only features poets like Shakespeare but it also focuses on contemporary poets like Joni Mitchell and her song 'Woodstock'. Voted one of the top 100 public intellectuals by Foreign Policy and Prospect magazines, Paglia is a media celebrity, appearing on television and radio in the United States and internationally. Her column at Salon.com is compulsive reading.*

I had arranged to interview Paglia at Harry's Seafood Grill in Wilmington, Delaware—her choice. I got to Harry's early and knocked back a shot of tequila to settle my nerves—Paglia's renowned spontaneity can be challenging for interviewers. She was smaller than I expected but still larger than life. I find it refreshing that Paglia says what she thinks, uncensored, a habit that often puts people on edge. And I'm happy to report that after the interview, my girl crush is intact.

CA In *Break, Blow, Burn* you critique those who have undermined poetry. Who are these people?

PAGLIA Well, the first half of *Break, Blow, Burn* is essentially concerned with canonical work and most people would not disagree with the kinds of choices that I have made. However, in the second half, which addresses the last four decades, with the exceptions of Sylvia Plath, Gary Snyder, and Joni Mitchell (for *Woodstock*), no one is a known name. The contemporary section of this book is really a slap in the face of the current poetry establishment and academic circles, in the sense that I have not included poets who are approved by the academy. These days, this would include John Ashbery, for example, who is glorified and considered a genius in the United States. I have no doubt that he had talent once but I find his poems unreadable and pretentious. To me they are a knock-off of late Wallace Stevens. I love early Wallace Stevens, but the late period is so abstruse and philosophical—or rather academics have reduced the late Wallace Stevens to this philosophical poet. What follows from this is the idea that somehow people write poetry to do philosophy. Well, I say, 'Do philosophy! Don't treat poetry as if it was a servant of some other form.'

Jorie Graham is glorified as if she is a deep thinker, as if she is a philosopher 'interrogating' the meanings of words—what absolute rubbish! Again, she is someone who may have had talent once, but why is she teaching at Harvard? Because her poetry dovetails beautifully with the sterile postmodernism of the academic elite. But now postmodernism is ebbing, and all the careerist academics with their fingers in the wind are fleeing like lemmings and moving back to the more traditional genres. Jorie Graham is a flack—a time-server and sycophant. That's how you get yourself a job at Harvard—you simply mirror back to the academics around you their particular current little interest or concern. I come out of the sixties and my philosophy of poetry is that it is based in the senses; I think that is the essence of poetry. The essence of the sixties revolution was sensory—a sensory turn back to the senses. Poetry is different from philosophy in the way that it plays upon our senses. Whether it's through rhythm, through imagery, through the tactility of words, it is arousing elements of the brain that are pre-rational, and this is interacting with our neurology. So it's like we're floating on a green river of some sort.

For me, poetry has got to play to the senses in some way. That's why the Shakespeare sonnets have lasted. It's not so much because he is a master of language, it's that he is a true poet who is oriented towards the physical world, processing himself through his body and coming out his mouth. He endorses the idea of poetry as a purely pleasurable exercise.

Break, Blow, Burn got very good reviews, but there were a few really nasty ones. Some of them were political, but there was one that said that I didn't deal with really difficult poetry like that of Jorie Graham, and that I needed to deal with her. Jorie Graham! Haven't they read the book? I didn't mention her by name, but I dismissed her style of poetry. In many ways the arts have hit a dead end partly because of this trend in poetry.

CA Why else have the arts hit a dead end?

PAGLIA The world listens to media, young people listen to the media. It used to be an American phenomenon but now we see it everywhere. The traditional arts are suffering and being marginalised out of the utter folly that began in academe in the seventies. The post-sixties revolution suddenly started gearing towards postmodernism with its repercussions of language. It is slippery, self-reflective language and is full of contortions—native English speakers are imitating bad English translations of French intellectuals. If you are French, you can get away with that (the French need to interrogate themselves; they have a very rationalist culture). But what Lacan is doing in French can't be replicated in English—and we don't need it in English. My argument has been that our tradition of poetry runs all the way back to English-speaking poetry—to Chaucer. I said early on in my manifesto that everything Foucault claims to be doing is already done in Joyce's *Ulysses* and is done far better: all you need is that book. It is an outrage to see these English professors of my generation trot out this language, like Stephen Greenblatt who sees Foucault as a brilliant man. I mean, you have a very empty head to be that fascinated with Foucault. It's warfare! I don't know if you know how ostracised I am in American academe? I hope you realise. Greenblatt started out at Yale several years ahead of me in grad school. He has carefully erased certain things from his biography. There is a book where he talks about the way he was a rebel in taking a non-literary approach at Yale, but he avoids saying that he won the John Addison Porter Prize for the best dissertation in the Yale graduate school. In other words, he was the apple of his professors' eyes. My own dissertation, *Sexual Personae*, was not even allowed to be considered for the Porter Prize, even though there was no limit on how many dissertations could be put forward by any department. Greenblatt's book on Shakespeare (*Will in the World*) is a mess—shockingly so, in my view. I think the only reason it did well is because of that nice drawing of Shakespeare on the front! As someone who has taught and written about Shakespeare for my whole career, I simply don't recognize Greenblatt's Shakespeare—whom he turns into a nebulous version of himself. He reduces *Hamlet* to the minor issue of Shakespeare's son, Hamnet, and is overly concerned about fathers and daughters in the play. And then he makes a big deal about Shakespeare going to London and supposedly getting traumatized by a head on a pike. What is he talking about? It was hundreds of years ago, for heaven's sake. People were slaughtered all the time. You had chickens, pigs, deer constantly being slaughtered in the backyard. There was butchery everywhere, dead bodies everywhere. Greenblatt, the New Historicist, has a very narrow and anachronistic view of history. Yet he is the crème de la crème of American academe. That says everything, doesn't it? Who is the real rebel? Stephen Greenblatt who glided from Yale to Berkeley to Harvard—or me, who has paid the price? Headhunted professors at those elite institutions are millionaires. And look at the pack of secretaries and graduate student assistants around them. I don't have any of that here. At the University of the Arts I have a very small staff, so I rely on other people to help me. My agent helps me, my publisher helps me and a few others do my email and so on, but I have no clerical assistants of any kind. And I believe that is more what an intellectual should be. An intellectual should be someone who is outside the system and also who can't be categorised neatly. But these people are like rajas.

CA What can be done to restore and nurture a love of poetry?

PAGLIA There is a terrible problem in America: there has been a drift away from the visibility of poetry in education or even for the daily reader of newspapers and magazines. When I was growing up in the fifties and early sixties, even women's magazines had poetry editors. I saw poems in the daily newspaper. I remember them and they were often very general with lines like 'Oh, the red leaves' or whatever, but poetry was still very central to American culture then. People used to be able to recite poetry, and mass media has supplanted that. Obviously, people don't sit around strumming banjos as much as they used to in America. Song is not a form of family entertainment at family parties the way it used to be, where people would sing or play an instrument. (That's not so in Ireland—song is still very much a part of their culture.) It's gone here because of the dominance of the media.

The problem is also in the way poetry was taught. The kind of poetry that I was introduced to in high school in the early sixties was completely sanitised; poetry was ruined for me. If I had been a poet then, it would have just made me want to scream. I thought it was totally fake—everything about it was fake. The way that the poetry of Emily Dickinson was taught meant that if I had not read Emily Dickinson in college, I would have had the most saccharine ideas about Dickinson's poetry. I was taught it was all about little things like birds and bees and butterflies and so on and so forth. That is why I wrote my chapter on 'Amherst's Madame de Sade: Emily Dickinson'; I had to chop down those ideas about her poetry. I was lucky that I was around at the time that the new Harvard University edition of her poems by Thomas Johnson was published. It was the edition that reinstated the dashes in her poems. I was really the first generation to use that, so Dickinson has been an enormous presence for me since college.

Poetry needs to be taught and restored to the curriculum. It's quite wrong that there is this namby-pamby politically correct humanitarian thing that is being taught now. I also think the visual arts need to be taught to American school children. In Europe the visual arts are all around young people, they are a part of the European heritage. Here there is nothing. If you do not talk to students or present art to them, they see nothing—nothing but shopping malls and special effects in movies. I wrote an essay about this called 'The Magic of Images'. I posit that visual culture has been bombarded with 'flash, flash, flash, flash, flash,' and it is no longer done with the skill of Godard who invented that style. He was a brilliant filmmaker. Now it's being done by copyists. It's now become just crazy images that don't make any sense.

Kids are being bombarded—they are looking at TV and going to movies and 'flash, flash flash'—their visual sense is disrupted. We have to retrain the brain. Kids need to be trained to look; an encounter of the eye with a single image should be explored. Whether it is a photograph, a great painting, or whatever it is, just sit there and stare at it and explore it with the eye. No wonder kids have attention deficit disorder and are living on Ritalin in this country. We have to get great images into the elementary schools and even into the college curriculum. In our wonderfully pc academe, the great art history survey courses are being dismantled everywhere. In the Larry Summers controversy at Harvard, one of the things that was mentioned in the media was that he tried to bring back the art history survey course—he thought undergraduates needed that. An unnamed woman, an art historian there (I'm guessing it was Svetlana Alpers, but I don't know) said to him, 'No true professor would ever teach that course.' But these courses are for the betterment of undergraduates!

My sister, who is an art conservator, went to Smith College. She went on a rampage, a crusade, when Smith started to dismantle its art history survey because no one wanted to teach it. There was an outcry from Smith graduates. People who were lawyers, who were science majors, all said it was the best course they took at Smith College. It was the most memorable course they had undertaken.

I am so much in favour of the survey (another way in which I am out of sync with academic trends). My book, *Sexual Personae*, is set out like a survey course. It is the same thing with *Break, Blow Burn*. And that approach is out of favour. There is no sequence, there is no chronology in new approaches. You are expected to structure things like New Historicism, where you take this little fact and this little fact [she makes small tweezers-like movements] and put them together like a tiny little salad. Then you pick at it and these little facts fit together. Fit together my ass!

Stephen Greenblatt is not erudite. None of them is of the dimensions that their predecessors were, like Harry Levin, Emily Vermeule. The Ivy League was once known for great scholars. These current scholars are careerists. None of them is truly original. They all like talking about what is current in the environment and then they find another new trend and say, 'I'll base my career on it and get rich.' And they do get rich!

CA What do you think about postmodernist jargon overtaking various other disciplines at the university?

PAGLIA On my book tours people tell me how they were driven out of the universities. For example, in Kansas City a woman told me she was doing a graduate year in public administration and she had to read Foucault. This garbage has nothing to do with anything! People told me they left graduate school because of it; they wanted a career in literature but they were driven out by semantics. They were devastated. Everywhere parents are paying large sums of money in this country and their children are being forced to read jargon. There was a scandal when a parent went to the press after spending all this money to send his daughter to film school in California and she was forced to read valueless jargon. When she complained, she was told, 'Oh, please, you simply aren't capable of understanding it!'

When I wrote the book on *The Birds*, there were some reviews that said, 'This book does nothing', and they said that because it focuses on the film. That's the point. It's not about stupid jargon; it's about the film. Laura Mulvey is a very nice person but Mulvey's writing of the 'male gaze' is like ivy or bamboo—you can never get rid of it. What does she know about the visual arts? She has no business talking about the 'male gaze' in regards to a genre without having explored these ideas in relationship to the whole history of the visual arts. Feminists like her apply a rubber stamp to whatever they are arguing in any genre. Film is a development of Western visual art. That's why in *Sexual Personae* I'm talking about what I call the 'Western Eye', which is used by both male and female in Western culture. It's not just the 'male gaze'!

That kind of ideological thinking has ruined feminism.

When I burst on the scene in the nineties I was treated really badly. Gloria Steinem compared me to Hitler, and my book—which she obviously hadn't read—she compared to *Mein Kampf*. This is the way you treat an openly gay woman in the movement? Anyway, thanks to Madonna, we won. (Thank you, Madonna!)

The pro-sex team won—pro-beauty, pro-art, pro-fashion, pro-pop. All that stuff won! But now from the new younger feminists, all we hear is, 'Oh, these terrible model competitions and wet t-shirt contests!' They complain, complain, complain.

CA Do you think that poetry is more magical than prose?

PAGLIA Yes. Absolutely. Poetry descends from the sacred. There is always a remnant of the sacred, even in people who are atheists and write poetry. There is something about this cosmic vision that allows you to view the universe in its totality. Art gives you an attention to the fine detail, a sharpening of the power of observation. Art gives you the ability to see your ordinary life in a different way—the ordinary becomes extraordinary. Poetry is a form of heightened consciousness. It is analogous to how people feel when they are in love or when they are drinking or when they are on drugs. I don't take drugs but I am a child of the vine. (And I also like a beer). Postmodernism has marginalised poetry because postmodernism is a type of cynical nihilism. It defines any reference to the sacred as sentimental. There is a kind of sanctimonious superiority that many postmodernist scholars have, regarding what people believe.

I'm very interested in all religions, and I think that every religion is a symbol system that is coherent in itself. Higher education should teach comparative religion. When you bring religions together and compare them, they are like great poems. Through that, you actually see the way the universe exists—so many different views of the vastness of the cosmos.

To return to my earlier remark, postmodernism is cynical—it is a little, snivelling way of seeing the world; it actually follows from the movement created by T. S. Eliot in 'The Waste Land' and Samuel Beckett in *Waiting for Godot*. Postmodernism and poststructuralism are part of the heritage of Beckett. Foucault himself said the biggest influence on his generation in Paris was Samuel Beckett's *Waiting for Godot*. Susan Sontag spent much of her life trying to bring us back to that world of *Waiting for Godot*. When she went over to Sarajevo, what did she do? She produced *Waiting for Godot* in the rubble! I acknowledge it is a great play of the twentieth century and one must know it. But I utterly reject Samuel Beckett's vision of the world. No one seems to notice that, first of all, there are no women in *Waiting for Godot*. Hello! Wouldn't you think there is something wrong there? That is not a universal vision. When you have a major playwright like that excluding women, then wouldn't the interpretation be that women are the problem? Hobos along the roadside picking at chicken bones? I hate that. But that is the sensibility everywhere of postmodernism, the 'abject'—all that stuff. Give me a break. It has been done. It is has been *so* done. Get rid of it! It is passé. My sensibility is that of my generation, the sixties, the psychedelic sixties of rock and roll and 'Satisfaction' and Andy Warhol.

CA Why do you think texts like *Waiting for Godot* are taught so prominently in universities?

PAGLIA Because the real vision, unfortunately, got truncated. Because my generation went off on that psychedelic era. Although I have never taken any of those drugs, I feel I'm part of psychedelia because of the music. It can give you a sense of what it's like to be on drugs. Some of my favourite music is drug music but yet I don't take drugs. Part of the problem with my generation is that people who could have prevented this terrible thing that happened in academia did not go on to grad school. They dropped like flies. They took drugs. They died of AIDS. Two of my friends died of AIDS. One of my subjects is the self-destruction of my generation. I wrote an article about it: 'Cults and Cosmic Consciousness: Religious Vision in the American 1960s'. That is the real sixties. Don't tell me that it's Foucault sitting someplace in Paris hearing about the revolution on the telephone.

If you are a practitioner, an exponent of the humanities, and you are getting the salaries that those people are getting at Harvard and Berkeley, how dare you smash the humanities the way they have done! How dare you be so snobbish about art! How dare you ruin the experience of literature by stripping away the magic and the sacred! That is what they have done. I had great luck to have the poet Milton Kessler as a teacher when I was in college at the State University of New York at Binghamton. He was always bringing into class readings that he had discovered which had something to do with the relationship between the body and poetry. He had studied with Roethke. And Roethke is now marginalized. People have written to me thanking me for trying to bring back Roethke. Why is Roethke out? Because he is about the body and the sacred. Are undergraduates really reading Jorie Graham and not Roethke?

The New York Times asked me to weigh in when Larry Summers resigned as president of Harvard. It's hilarious because there I was, at the small University of the Arts, telling Harvard what it should do. And Harvard worships *The New York Times*; it was a wonderful piece of effrontery. The guy who commissioned it was the same one who commissioned my original Madonna piece for *The Times* in 1990, David Shipley. He later met and married Naomi Wolf; they are now divorced. I cannot authenticate this, but I heard via the grapevine back then that they met because of that Madonna piece. Naomi's uncle (her mother's brother) worked at *The Times*, and when they published that piece she marched into the editorial office and told Shipley that *The Times* should not be publishing Camille Paglia. Evidently, sparks flew between them, and one thing led to another. Soon they were dating, and then they were married and had two children—I should be the godmother! If it's true, it's a good example of the way Naomi still works—pretending to be a woman of the people but always the careerist working the system and pulling strings from behind the scenes. Anyway, he's well rid of her now.

I have often said that Naomi and Susan Faludi suffered terribly from their deficient Ivy League education. These women are smart, but they have unformed minds. They have no general knowledge; the way they were educated is a scandal. It's truly a scandal that Naomi Wolf graduated from Yale yet writes as slackly as she does. At the start at least, her work was heavily edited. *The New Republic* once published a debate between her and me in stages. It went back and forth, so that each of us would reply to the other. I said to the editor, 'My god—look at her prose, you've got to print this as is!' But they wouldn't print it—they edited it for their readers. With her first book, *The Beauty Myth*, she got a lot of help behind the scenes. Her father is a writer and a close friend of a famous agent, and they worked her material into shape before publication. With me it's a one-woman operation; what you see is what you get.

CA Dana Gioia said you write beautifully; that you have written the perfect sentence.

PAGLIA Thank you very much for conveying that; but of course, Gioia isn't an academic, that's why he can feel free to say that. I appreciate hearing that. He has a sense of the crusade that I do. He has a very keen sense of the general culture, unlike the academics at Harvard. He is not a snob like they are. He doesn't think his clientele are the best of the best—like Harvard, for example. I mean, give me a break! When these Harvard grads emerge nowadays as journalists in the media, for example, they reveal just how badly educated they are. Their poor parents bankrupted themselves for their children's education. Gioia has a very accurate sense of the state of popular culture without any of the claptrap that you find in the way popular culture is taught in academe—like the Frankfurt School. Susan Faludi is a victim of that stuff, where everything is about 'commodification' in the Marxist sense. They see the relationship between popular culture and the mass audience as pure power over passivity. In their view, the poor empty-headed mass audience is constantly led astray by a wicked, conspiratorial elite somewhere—Hollywood or New York or wherever. What a stupid way to view popular culture! All Hollywood has ever been from the start is a bunch of people looking at every success and asking, 'How can we imitate it?' They will go straight to where the dollars are—they completely subordinate themselves to the audience and its tastes. The commentary on popular culture is so distorted, sanctimonious and superior. And there are real problems with popular culture. But they can't be remedied by Marxist academics, because they don't understand it.

But Dana Gioia gets the rhythm and dynamic of popular culture, like I do. Maybe it has something to do with him being part Italian. My family were immigrants; all four of my grandparents and my mother were born in Italy, and they came to the U.S. to work in a shoe factory. My father became a high school teacher and then a college teacher, but none of his many brothers and sisters went to college. So I am always oriented towards public education. That is why I try to write in an accessible manner, not in that pernicious post-modern jargon. Every defence of that style as 'important' was nonsense! Most of the key people in that fad are about to retire, and they will certainly be enjoying the fat pensions that they accumulated by writing that drivel. It's so absurd that those elitist careerists were considered Leftist—when the real rebels were the ones who refused to write like that.

CA Harold Bloom supervised your thesis—do you still have a relationship with him?

PAGLIA I was never a part of his court. I'm not part of anyone's court. I am my own person. Bloom came from a large family originally, so he's created an enormous extended family around himself consisting of his current and former students. There are always people hanging around and doing things for him. I have stayed away from all of that—it's just not my thing. But when Naomi Wolf charged Bloom with sexual harassment in *New York* magazine and *The New York Observer* contacted me for comment, I defended him. He sent me a very nice letter scrawled in his hand which said, 'You are my beloved daughter in whom I am well pleased.'

I told them that Naomi has spent her life batting her eyes and bobbing her boobs in the face of men, and I said, 'How long must we relive your adolescence, Naomi? How many times will you return to your teenage years?' (I was using the rhetorical device of apostrophe, which I learned in high school from Cicero's oration against Catiline—'How long will you continue to abuse our patience?') I appealed to Naomi, 'Please move on to menopause!' The thing is, whatever her charges were, if she didn't have the courage to bring them forward at the time, then she shouldn't have done it twenty-one years later in a cover story of *New York* magazine. And *New York* had no right to simply give over its pages to unsubstantiated accusations. If there was a story there, then it should have been assigned it to a real reporter to investigate and get comments from other people, not just Naomi.

For example, I have told people many times that there were a lot of sexual affairs going on between married male professors and women students when I was in graduate school. I saw no problem with it at the time—I viewed it as a matter of free choice. In the long run, however, it does seem as if the women who were involved in those relationships have had successful careers but nevertheless difficulty in establishing their own independent voices as critics. I'm not sure if this was already signaled in their willingness to have the affairs in the first place. In many ways it was useful for me to be a lesbian—even though I had no sex life! I was the only openly gay person at Yale Graduate School, which I entered in 1968, a year before Stonewall.

CA That's very brave.

PAGLIA You bet it was, and it cost me. When it came time for job interviews, it's no coincidence that one of my friends had twelve job offers while I had none. It looked like I would be jobless until at the end of my last year at Yale, Bennington College had a sudden opening, and they called Harold Bloom and asked, 'Is there anyone good left?' That's how I finally got hired. Marjorie Garber, by the way, was one of the many closeted people at Yale. She cut off her relationship with me because I was too open in my behaviour. She curtly told me, 'It won't do!' Career advance was her top priority. She had nothing to do with feminism at the time either. She finally came out as a lesbian when it was safe—fifteen years later in the '80s.

Anyway, Harold Bloom has become a well-known, beloved figure and has done an enormous amount for opening up public interest in classic literature. But I wish that he had spent more time addressing the problem of post-modernism and post-structuralism, which he dismisses but says nothing about. That's my complaint about him. He has not played a leadership role in the profession.

CA I wanted to ask you about creative writing in universities—should it be there? Can you teach creative writing?

PAGLIA I think it is a double-edged sword. On the one hand, in a culture that is often media-driven, the people who go into graduate programs in creative writing are finding a little island where arts and letters are taken seriously. They have a connection not only with knowledgeable teachers who can help in their careers but also with fellow students who can be friends for a lifetime, corresponding with them and so on. At university writers find fellow thinkers, they find encouragement, they find others who take writing seriously. On the other hand, sometimes a house style is imposed.

On my book tours I'm often asked whether writers should study creative writing at universities. My advice to young writers is that if you want to teach and earn a living while writing, then you have to be credentialed and get your degree in these programs. But if you don't want to teach but really write, I don't think it's a good idea. I think that you should take that money and use it to give yourself some other experience. To travel—to Asia, to Africa, India—anywhere. Or give yourself a gap year, something like that. Writing profits from life experience, and if you never have any experience other than that in a classroom, then your writing is inevitably going to become rarefied and artificial. You are in a bubble. Why preserve this academic bubble? Hardly any of the great writers ever had academic careers. They had to live life, whatever it was. It's far better to go out and get an ordinary job, if you can. People watching is important; you need to people watch.

There is a kind of a removal from life in a writing program, and the materials that you need for writing are not going to be found in academe. Your technical skills may be polished, but you have to look to life itself and all the experiences in life as fodder for writing. Unfortunately, middle-class people have very little contact with real jobs anymore. I remember when the musician David Amram came to The University of the Arts to speak. He lived through the beatnik era. He said that then, if you wanted to write poetry, you wanted to make music, you wanted to dance, rents were cheap, and you were living ten to a room. And if you needed money, you would all go out and varnish floors for a job—you'd pick up a day job. Or you would unload trucks for a day. Now, where in American culture right now are you going to find that? People say, 'I'll wait on tables or work in an office. but I don't want to varnish floors. I don't want to unload trucks.' That's the difference, and that's why that Beat movement was truly representative of the fifties and early sixties.

They were middle class, but they went backwards in their class. They looked like bums with their beards and all that. And as bums they actually saw and experienced things that were outside of their class. That's one of the problems right now—the whole culture is shifting to become much more middle class. Americans now are incredibly desirous of brand names for every single thing. I was shopping for a new perfume recently and when I asked for a sample I was told, 'You can't sample them.' I said, 'How will I know what to buy if I don't smell them?' For young people, the brand name is enough on the perfume. They buy the brand name, not the scent of the perfume. I loved it when Warhol came out with the Campbell's soup can. I loved that—I love brand names and logos. But with Warhol, the interest in the design and logo of a simple Campbell's soup can was populist. This new trend is simply about seeking the prestige of the name brand. In the ghetto, people are killing each other over brand name sneakers. So something has gone very wrong in the culture.

Materialism destroys the artist. The lives of the artists are very inspiring. But they weren't people of power as some people argue—that is ridiculous. Most of them were complete losers. Dante was a loser. Hardly anyone born to wealth and power has been a great artist.

Of course there are exceptions, like James Merrill (although I'm not a fan of his work). He's from money and has the Merrill fortune behind him. But he was gay and therefore he was an outsider and a loser in his culture.

I despise it when I hear people argue that we need to revamp our canon to bring in things from the margins. But to produce great work, you nearly always had to work from the margins! That is why the authorship argument about Shakespeare—the Oxford hypothesis or the Bacon hypothesis that no one but a nobleman could have written his plays—is nonsense. When have the nobility ever been able to produce great or important art? OK, Toulouse Lautrec was from the nobility, but he was an outcast because of his disability. Other than that, where? Who? No major artist has ever come from nobility.

CA Has the reading of literature declined? Are people still reading classics?

PAGLIA I don't think people are reading classics. There is too much competition, too much going on—video game culture (especially for young men in America), movies, TV, iPods, the web. The web is a major transformation—people are reading but a different kind of reading. In America, at least, there are a very small number of people actually reading classics. Except for students in college—if the classics and reading haven't been ruined for them.

When I began my teaching career at Bennington College, coming out of grad school at Yale in 1972, I assigned the same number of readings as I had read at Yale; which was a novel a week. Two weeks into the term, one of the professors took me aside and said, 'We really don't do things in that way here. We prefer deep reading instead; that much reading is too much for them.' So I adjusted down to one novel every three weeks, and over time—over 40 years of teaching—I have given up finding a long book that students will read. I just can't stand to police students—they are not going to read a 700-page book. At the University of the Arts I don't have any majors. My students are majoring in theatre or animation or whatever. They have to please their master teachers and think about a different kind of career. So I can tell when they haven't read the book. I have seen the way a class becomes duplicitous where they think they have to hide from you that they haven't done the reading. But if I *was* teaching the English major to someone at university intending to get into grad school, then those students would read that 700-page book and think about their professional careers!

So I slowly reduced the amount of outside reading I assigned them and I upped the ante of what was going on in class. I try to make it really intense in class when I have them. And that is why I found that poems work well. I can force them to read a poem and even a play. But even in my Shakespeare class, I can tell that they are not reading—many are, but I can tell which students aren't. With Shakespeare you have to make a hard sell. I would say that most students at Harvard or Princeton do the reading, but I think faculty there are fooling themselves, too.

There are so many things kids want to be doing and the web is an enormous part of that. To try and get them to the library and open a book—why should they, when they are used to being online all night? Why would they go to the library when they could do this online? I began writing for *Salon.com* from its first issue in 1995, so I am committed to the web.

Even I find it easier to look for facts if I can find a reliable source on the web. I don't have to get up out of my seat, cross the room, pull out my *Oxford Classical Dictionary* (the older edition, never the new one, which is riddled with postmodernism—the new academics and the new scholarship are totally unreliable).

It's such an effort, isn't it?—to get up, open the book, find what you're looking for in the book. It's a crisis. A major, major crisis is happening. I don't think it can be stopped. The whole new generation worldwide is choosing the web, and books are becoming a joke. But here's the problem: the web is a very convenient way to do work.

If I were writing *Sexual Personae* again, it would be so easy to be able to key in a word and access a whole library of stuff. But it wouldn't be *Sexual Personae* at the end of it. *Sexual Personae* is the result of someone who immersed herself in books, sat there at the Yale library, took books off the shelves and roamed and roamed, looking, looking, looking.

You're not going to do that now. The ability of the web to go straight to what you are looking for has changed this process. You don't have a book in your hands, so you can't flip through it to the other things that are in the book. I find so many things—incredible things—in the library just by walking through it and looking for something else.

No-one wants to go to the library anymore. You can get the information on the web, but the act of acquiring the information and the networking connections of information are very different. The web is great for helping you to trace things; it's fabulous—I love it for that. It's addictive. But no one is ever again going to want to open an encyclopaedia, as I did. I used a Columbia Encyclopaedia, a one-volume thing that I owned and used extensively throughout my college years and grad school. I used to open it up and study it, and I would stumble onto other things in it and keep reading and keep going. My general knowledge comes from books like that.

The people of the book—my era—can see what is going to be lost, but it is unstoppable. Something else is happening. Prose style will suffer because you only get prose style by reading consecutively. People have said, 'You are very readable', and that's because my writing flows. That's the result of years and years of consecutive reading. If you don't read consecutively, you will never have flow. You might juxtapose things in an interesting way, but you will be just sampling things—people become samplers. Over time people and knowledge will suffer from this kind of sampling until people begin reading the past once more. I believe in that—you look at the past and you are inspired and start going to the library again. Things are lost but ultimately they are recovered.

CA Who are your role models?

PAGLIA When I was growing up in upstate New York, I had no role models—there weren't any in the domestic '50s. So I went to the past and found role models in earlier women like Amelia Earhart. At a second-hand bookstore, I found some paperbacks by Mary McCarthy with her photo on them. She was a great inspiration to me. Dorothy Parker was another one—I read her witticisms and stories about her life in the '20s. Simone de Beauvoir was important to me as an intellectual. Much later, I saw a parallel in Joni Mithcell's background because she grew up on a prairie. It was a bit how I felt in upstate New York in the Snow Belt. There was gorgeous scenery, but it was very isolated.

When I write, I always try to write for it to be re-read. It's not just for now. I am imagining someone in the future discovering me in a library, just as I discovered the writers who influenced me. I feel like I've learnt from the masters. I love Oscar Wilde, for example. At the same second-hand bookstore, I stumbled on what became one of my most important books, *The Epigrams of Oscar Wilde.* (It's still in print, but it's been re-titled, *The Wit and Humour of Oscar Wilde*—I guess the American publisher felt no one would know what 'epigram' means!) This became a bible to me in high school. All of Wilde's witticisms were divided into categories like

Art, Nature, Men and Women. He wrote stunning one-liners. That is what I try to do. I focus on the single sentence and try to make it as strong as possible, so that it can be quoted. This makes my sentences portable. Think about Susan Sontag, who's supposedly so brilliant—try to find a single quotable sentence. Okay, so there was, 'The white race is the cancer of history', but she renounced it! The discipline of the one-liner is a great exercise in writing. How much can you pack into a single sentence?

CA What are your current projects? Isn't there a plan to write a second volume of *Sexual Personae*?

PAGLIA Pantheon will release my new book on the visual arts in Fall 2012, and I have a third essay collection also under contract to Pantheon. I haven't abandoned the *Sexual Personae* project, but developments in the 1990s made me radically re-think it. Popular culture has become ubiquitous—but it has also declined in quality. The Web has enamoured the young and drained a great deal of creative energy from movies, TV, and rock music. (I speak as a proponent of the Web, not its critic.) As a consequence, (and to my regret) volume two will inevitably have an elegiac character—it will be chronicling something that is already gone with the wind. And as a strategic matter, it may very well be the last book I write!—a summa of my love affair with pop.

Paglia emailed me a letter a week after the interview. It was a really interesting letter, a kind of de-briefing but also a personal response to our meeting. She provided addenda to a few of the points she had made in the interview, asked me to share more of my experiences with her and even commented on how apt it was that Suicide Blonde had been playing in the restaurant (given that I am Australian). She tells me: 'I'm serious about calling it a masterpiece of pop culture—the music, lyrics, and eerily hypnotic sonic distortions. I rank it with Chaka Khan's "Ain't Nobody" (see my Disco Playlist), which I've also called a masterpiece.'

'Deeper Resonances'
Paul Kane

There is a stanza in Paul Kane's poem, 'Shadow', that haunts me:

> As the wake pursues the boat, the water
> Enfolds the sky in the well of the waves.
> You drink the light in, as you would the air,
> In deep breaths, in dilations of time.
> *And do you know what it is to live?*

From the time I read it in Kane's book, Drowned Lands, *it has been on the edge of my consciousness. It somehow reminds me of some of Gwen Harwood's poems, especially 'Iris'. I was first introduced to Kane's work when I was writing my PhD on Harwood's pseudonymous poetry. I devoured his book,* Australian Poetry: Romanticism and Negativity, *in the first few months of my candidature. It confirmed my view that poets make the best poet-critics. I remember taking a photocopy of his chapter on Gwen Harwood, cleverly entitled 'Capable Negativity', to my supervision meeting and I learnt that Kane was a friend of my supervisor, Chris Wallace-Crabbe. In fact, perhaps in response to discussions of transcendentalism pervading their poetry, Kane and Wallace-Crabbe invented a group called the Descendentalists, whose doctrines Wallace-Crabbe claims are 'inscrutable, tone jocular'. Kane adds that, 'The Descendentalist Club early on had a newsletter (two issues, 1995 and 1996. There's lots to say about it, but I don't know how much is fit to print.' The Descendentalists would meet at Universita (an Italian restaurant in Lygon street, Carlton, near The University of Melbourne) 'twice or thrice a year'. I think of Kane as an honorary Australian: he studied at The University of Melbourne, was a Fulbright Scholar to Australia in 1984–5 and had even taught at Monash University. It is not surprising then, that one of Kane's research specialisations is Australian and post-colonial literature.*

Kane is currently Professor of English and Co-Associate Chair of English at Vassar College, Poughkeepsie, New York. He writes books, essays, reviews and poems. It is hard to say whether I enjoy his poetry or criticism more; they are both beautifully written and often stirring. Educated at Yale, Kane has been awarded an impressive array of grants and fellowships. These include fellowships from the National Endowment for the Humanities and the John Simon Guggenheim Memorial Foundation, as well as grants from the Australia Council, the Bienecke Foundation, and the Andrew W. Mellon Foundation. He has been poetry editor of Antipodes *since 1987 and was one of the first editors to accept my work for publication in a literary journal. Kane has also served as Artistic Director of the annual Mildura Writers Festival since 2002 and has a house in rural Victoria.*

I met Paul at the staff club, University House, at The University of Melbourne. It is the only interview I undertook in Australia. It was noisy at 'the House' and so we found a little corner in one of the lounges to talk. Paul is softly spoken and I wanted to make sure that the recording picked up the cadence of his voice, which I would describe as soothingly intellectual—if that's not an oxymoron. His passion for poetry is fierce; he knows what it is to live.

CA What do you think is the future of poetry? Dana Gioia questions its survival in its current form.

KANE I wouldn't agree with him on that, though perhaps it depends on what you mean by 'current form'. I imagine he is wondering about such developments as Slam poetry and the public base of it. Is that the future? I expect poetry is going to go in the way it has been going, in a myriad of directions, and will survive in many different forms. Perhaps the more literary forms will be less honoured in the academy, but then Richard Howard, the poet/critic, thinks poetry should really become a kind of closet vice, you should hide it away, you shouldn't admit you do it. He is utterly opposed to the idea that April is a poetry month, for instance, or that we need some large public display of affection for it. Of course, he is taking the matter in a contrarian direction. I'm not quite that extreme but I appreciate the impulse: there is so much variety in poetry that it will find its channels; it has survived a long time and will continue to survive.

CA What is the responsibility of a public intellectual and how do you think the role of the public intellectual has changed over time?

KANE I suppose you would have to begin by making a distinction between those we regard as pundits, or experts in an area, and those who work as academics in a particular field. I would regard a public intellectual as someone who rises out of a specific field, where there is a sense of expertise standing behind that figure, and who is then able to take a large step into a different arena where all the tools of intellectual investigation and thinking are applicable but in a wider context. There have been a lot of laments about the demise of the public intellectual of late. I think it reflects an exaggerated notion of the figure of the public intellectual in the past. I see them today as people like Noam Chomsky or a non-fiction writer such as Tony Judt. Susan Sontag was probably the preeminent one. In regards to what the role is, I think that it is largely an analytical one. Public intellectuals have to be able see the larger movements behind the events that are occurring in their culture and society and in the world. The public intellectual has some vision of the real import of events. Admittedly, that is a rare quality and the people who have the capacity need to be attended to. They're not exactly prophets but there is a sense in which they command respect.

CA Should the public intellectual work in the academy?

KANE It surely depends on the person. The academy in many ways, and I will say this about writers and poets as well, provides a form of patronage. Academia allows people—particularly in the U.S.—the freedom to do their work; within the context of the university, yes, but still with a good deal of latitude. So, I tend not to disparage universities, they have an important function, especially when they can harbour real intellectuals.

CA There have been discussions about how writing makes you a better teacher but does teaching make you a better writer/poet?

KANE It's a yes and a no. It does help one become better because you rarely understand what you read quite as thoroughly as when (a) you have written about it and (b) you have taught it. There is something about teaching that makes you work with literature in ways that you don't otherwise because suddenly you are trying to imagine it through the eyes of someone else and, in the discourse of the seminar, you are discovering things for yourself while also receiving continual feedback from students. Any teacher who is good, is learning as much as he or she is teaching.

When it comes to creative endeavours, however, I think there is a danger, and it is not the one that is most pointed to: the translation of literature into a dry academic milieu. It is more that in working on student writing one can begin to expend one's own creative energy on behalf of someone else. And I personally found that to be the case early on when I started doing some teaching in creative writing. I did come back to it years later because I began to understand how to avoid that problem. Teaching creative writing can affect you in a negative way, exhausting your powers.

CA Which Australian novelists and poets, if any, do you believe belong in the canon?

KANE Well, Australian literature is clearly under-represented in the so-called canon—there is no question about that if we are talking broadly about literature-in-English. I was speaking with Nicholas Jose today and he is putting together an anthology of Australian literature, which I think is modelled on the Norton anthologies of English and American literature, and, if it goes well, I imagine the book will have some of the same impact those anthologies have had. But because there hasn't been something like it before, which has endured and stayed in print, I think Australian writers are flying below the radar, particularly in the American academy. But I am hoping that Jose's book is going to help this profile.

It seems to me that Australian literature has slipped through a crack. British and American writing, of course, get the largest representation in the canon. And while Australia is part of postcolonial literature, which is getting increasingly play, it is a 'settler' literature like that of Canada and New Zealand, and therefore doesn't get the attention that the literatures of Africa and Asia and the Caribbean do, where matters of race and revolution are a driving force. Settler colonies, despite their indigenous populations, just don't have that kind of appeal to contemporary scholars. As a result, Australian literature is overlooked and it is something that I try to address in my own teaching in the States. So, in terms of the canon—a contested notion to be sure—Australian literature suffers from its in between position. There are a number of poets that I would like to see regarded as canonical, starting with some nineteenth and early twentieth-century poets and moving forward. I think Les Murray is going to be in there because he has that kind of world status already. But for other writers, like Gwen Harwood, it is going to take some work to get them a hearing. It doesn't just happen on its own, and Australia, as a nation, has to look to its cultural heritage as part of its international brief. With novelists it may be easier, you obviously have Patrick White, but also people like David Malouf and Henry Handel Richardson should have an impact eventually. Peter Carey is another. But it is a vast sorting out process and one doesn't really know how it will end up.

CA In what has been called the PlayStation age, are students still reading canonical texts? How important is this?

KANE At Vassar they are reading canonical texts because of the way we've structured the English major. And I think in the American academy, in general, you will find a lot of emphasis still on canonical literature. Is it important? Yes, I think it is.

CA Do the majority of students actually read the set texts on the curriculum?

KANE Speaking from my own experience, yes, and that is largely because of the liberal arts approach to tertiary education. For the most part, we conduct small seminars with the students and it is pretty clear when someone hasn't read something. Vassar is one of those highly selective colleges where you have a low student-to-faculty ratio and a significant amount of student contact. In the larger universities you don't have nearly as much, and the campus culture will be different. But for us, it isn't simply a matter of saying, okay you are responsible for this, and then wondering whether the students actually follow through. They are called to account much more. So I would say they are definitely reading. But there is another factor at work here. In the U.S. there is a kind of liberal ideology that has been debunked in many ways, and rather more successfully in Australia, I might add, but which continues to underwrite the public's idea of education. There is an anomaly at work in that American colleges and universities still espouse an idea of a liberal education that many of the professors probably don't agree with, but which society at large does. And because so much of private education is supported by donation—from loyal alumni, which is enormously important—that ideology necessarily remains intact, even though it may have been discredited. People still believe in the ideals of liberal education and are therefore willing to support the academy directly. In Australia, however, the critique has been so successful that it seems as if academics have talked themselves out of their jobs. That movement, of course, had a big push from the government, beginning with the disaster of the Dawkins reforms, and there is hardly any tradition of alumni giving to offset it.

CA Do poets make the best teachers of poetry in tertiary education?

KANE Well, it is helpful if the poet is a careful reader. I think a lot of poets who come in to talk about poetry are perfectly happy to speak about their own work but not necessarily about other work if they are expected to show expertise. I think even when you sit down to talk about your own poetry there is a sense that the person who wrote the poems is not exactly the same person talking about them. There is a sense of being a fraud, almost. This doesn't really stop writers from doing it and every poet has his or her notion of what they are about. Still, I do think that in the process of composing, one writes beyond one's own intelligence, and so when [poets] are thrown back upon their normal intelligence, they are probably not identical with the person who wrote originally. But one thing that poets can do is get across the aesthetic quality of writing, which students are hungry for. I suspect that in English courses in the U.S. we tell students one thing when we discuss writing critically or academically but send very different signals when we are teaching creative writing. And what happens is that much of the aesthetic experience that students look for, which animates their real interest in literature and writing, is to be found more often in the writing programmes than in the core curriculum. I think that imbalance is probably going to get addressed over time. Aesthetic considerations are going to become more central, alongside critical analysis and theory. It's just over the horizon, is my guess.

CA What is your view of postgraduate degrees in creative writing. Should they have a critical component?

KANE I would agree that there should be a critical component, especially if we are talking about a PhD, which has to be something categorically more than a Masters degree. In the U.S., the MFA is considered a terminal degree, the same as a PhD in an academic subject. But most of the programmes now are actually training readers more than writers. It is a little scary when you look at the number of programmes out there and consider the quantity of writers that are being certified, as it were, each year. You wonder what is going to become of them. They can't possibly all have a career in writing and you fear that the only career they can have is in teaching writing, and so it becomes a cycle or a robust feedback loop. But, at the same time, I do think that we are training readers and I hope that will encourage the literary culture. You often hear that more people write poetry than read it, which is a recipe for mediocrity to be sure. But I would not stand up and denounce the writing programmes because of mediocrity, not at all. You look at any age and there are always going to be lots of people writing, most of who will be mediocre. It has never been different and never will be.

CA How do you approach the teaching of poetry in analytical courses at Vassar?

KANE All of us at Vassar are still engaged in the close reading that is valorised in the New Critical movement, and which I think still has its place. I do ask my students often to read aloud and to memorise, which is something they enjoy. I approached that requirement initially with trepidation but found that students appreciate the opportunity to get poems by heart. At the same time, the emphasis is really on critical analysis. For me, it has to do with the capacity to write clearly and intelligently about poetry. That is the purpose of teaching it in an academic setting. It is also usually part of a larger effort or context, whether it be a survey course or a course on a specific period, and that will always have its own overarching concerns. But when it comes down to the teaching of the poems themselves it calls for what Nietzsche terms 'slow reading'. We move very slowly and carefully.

Just to jump over to the other side and address creative writing: it is always done in a small seminar setting. At the introductory level, which is in the second year, I sometimes teach a course in the writing of poetry. However, I don't do it as a workshop. I give them exercises and though they are meant to be producing original writing, we don't discuss it in class. We discuss instead the craft of poetry and we look at the nitty gritty elements, the nuts and bolts. I do meet with them individually and give them feedback since, really, they don't know enough in an introductory course to truly help one another. In the senior writing seminar, I do teach using workshops because, at that point, they have the training to comment helpfully on one another's work. But the introductory courses amount to a boot camp for poets, where they learn the technical requirements of rhyme, meter and form and other elements that you can clearly teach, since you can't teach creativity as such. I expect the students to know that technical material and to use it, even analytically. However, I don't demand they write formally in their own work, only that they learn how to do it and understand it in the poetry they encounter.

CA How do you compose your own poetry? From where do you get your inspiration?

KANE I think it generally starts with an impression. Sometimes it's the impression created by an event, by a conversation or another poet's writing, but it always has some quality to it that is arresting to me. And it seems as though that impression goes to another part of me that is like a poetic storehouse. Then it is really a matter of taking that impression and trying to work out from it. It is never the direct recounting of that impression because the impression is momentary, and there is always a gap between the origin of the poem and its beginning—that gap is never really closed. Poetry is always already after the fact. However, things do happen in the composition of a poem which sometimes feels like inspiration, though it often functions at the level of a word or phrase, rather than during an entire poem. It is what I was talking about before, of seeming to write beyond one's intelligence, where everything seems to come together and even a different quality of time emerges. So that is the ideal, I suppose. Most of the time, for me, the poem as a whole will come out in one or two sittings but then there is a lot of tinkering and a process of working to fulfil the poem's needs, rather than, let's say, my needs. I think it is a matter of working with what the poem wants to do, so there is kind of sensitivity that develops. Some poems can be heavily revised and yet maintain a direct relation to the initial impulse. With longer poems, that relationship can get more complicated. In general, most poems will be drafted in one sitting, but one sitting could be four hours or more.

CA How do you know when a poem is finished?

KANE Some poets say that it just clicks into place, and that does happen occasionally. Paul Valéry said famously that a poem is never finished, it is just abandoned, and there is certainly something to that because there comes a point in the revision of a poem where you have to know when to stop. I have ruined poems through too much revision and have been unable to repair them. Now, though, I have a pretty good sense of when I am finished with a poem, or vice versa.

CA How important is it to perform your work at festivals and readings? Do poets and writers now have to be performers to sell their books?

KANE There is a big emphasis on performance now and perhaps if there is a popular revival of poetry it will be because readings and performances have aided the resurgence. Not all poets are good performers of their material, and, while it probably isn't going to be crucial in the long run, people who present their work well are going to get larger audiences and reach more people initially. I think the main advantage is in the feedback you get when you read, you realise that poetry was always intended to be heard, it's the nature of language. I am very keen to have my poetry, not so much be accessible, as to have impact. My work tends to have a surface lucidity that depends upon inherent complexities so that the poems can be apprehended by a listener at a festival reading and, I hope, have a deeper resonance as well. I would say my poetry has improved through having performed my work. I've learned from others in this arena, too. But, to go back to your question, in terms of sales or perhaps careers, poets who frequently perform are probably going to do better.

CA I was reading about the Village College in Warwick and the way it connects local experts with interested people. That was in 2001. Was it successful?

KANE Right now it is on vacation or hiatus, but I did it for five years. It was a community learning project designed for the small village where I live, Warwick, about sixty miles northwest of New York. The place has attracted a lot of writers and artists and other creative people, and it seemed to me we could easily offer courses to the public at a price anyone could afford. I conceived it initially as a way people could give back to their community or at least share with the community something they had to offer. It came to me one day as an idea and at the time I was unhappy about it because I knew that it was such a good idea that it would have to be implemented. I didn't, however, think I was the right person to do it. The idea had come to the wrong person because I was something of a recluse. Still, I went to the local mayor and pitched the proposal to him to see what he thought. He's a young and dynamic fellow and he said you must do it. And so I began to network, which was unusual for me, and found so many talented and willing people that it really succeeded beyond what I expected, though not in the sense of success as large numbers or a lot of hoopla. It was a very quiet and intense kind of activity. It was congregated in the community, but was a free floating college with no fixed base. We held courses in wineries, bookstores, the library, in schools, wherever we could get a public space, and because it was so simple in concept and execution it was impossible for it to fail. The only way it could fail was if it got too large and, in fact, at one point it almost did and I had to scale it back. Finally, I turned it over to someone else but I may go back to it later. It was a wonderful thing to do and I learned a lot through the people I met and those who taught. We had a faculty that most colleges would have envied. We had three instructors who had Guggenheim fellowships, as well as NEH and NEA awards. It was a stellar faculty gathered simply from the people in the community. Most communities, I think, have such people.

CA I am very interested in your exploration of the Hudson Valley—how important is the principle of genius loci? Tell me a bit about the environmental studies course you offer at Vassar.

KANE That came about, in part, from a project that I did with a well-known photographer, William Clift. We did a book together called *A Hudson Landscape*. Clift is a photographer from New Mexico but had spent several years photographing the Hudson River Valley. After he finished, he asked if I would come aboard and write what we ended up calling, 'A Prose Companion', that was actually a kind of meditation on the Hudson Valley in its various guises. For me, it was a rediscovery of my connection with the area and its rich heritage. That led to teaching an experimental course in Vassar's Environmental Studies Program, called 'It's Only Natural: Contemplation in the American Landscape', which looked at the Hudson Valley but also a variety of other landscapes, including the American Southwest. I co-taught it with Mark Cladis, in the Religion Department, and we tried to use non-traditional modes of teaching, including lots of outside visitors and numerous field trips. And we brought in techniques of contemplation, which harkened back to early pre-Socratic and subsequent practices. Mark, who is now at Brown University, is writing a book about the course, which, I must say, makes me a little nervous, as it's bound to raise some eyebrows. But we had wonderful classes of discovery, and putting the course together was itself a mode of learning. I think for me teaching in non-traditional but appropriate ways is one possible future for education, given what our future looks like.

CA John Kinsella's book, *Fast, Loose Beginnings: A Memoir of Intoxications*, caused more than a ripple in the poetry world, and has even been dubbed a 'poetry war'. How do you feel about the writing of memoirs and specifically what Kinsella has done?

KANE I don't think such 'wars' help poetry, even if this one helps John's book as a side effect. I don't know the players all that well, though I do know John. It's a literary contretemps. It will pass, though it does, I suppose, point out the dangers of literary memoirs and of autobiographies or indeed biographies of living people. The undertaking is fraught with difficulty, particularly when you consider the way memory functions. People are simply not going to remember things in the same way, or even the same person in the same way twice. Reading about it in the papers, it just seems a flash in the pan. The recent controversy over the Patrick White hoax had more impact in shaking one's sense of the literary culture.

'They tend to seek me out' *Todd Gitlin*

The first thing you notice when you ask Todd Gitlin a question is the long pause that follows. At first it's a little intimidating and it would be easy to ramble into the space, except that if you make this mistake, you run the risk of missing Gitlin's pithy answer. The pause, I learnt, is Gitlin's way of composing the complexities and intricacies of his impending response. It's a pleasure to see his mind work.

Gitlin is a professor of journalism and sociology, and chair of the PhD program in communications, at Columbia University. He was head hunted by Columbia from New York University and prior to that he was a professor at the University of California, Berkeley. It reads like a dream run—except that Gitlin has worked hard for these kinds of opportunities. Not only does he have degrees in mathematics, political science and sociology from Harvard, the University of Michigan and Berkeley, respectively, in 1964–5 he was instrumental in the first national demonstration against the Vietnam War and was a coordinator of the SDS Peace Research and Education Project. He has written more than a dozen books including: The Sixties: Years of Hope, Days of Rage *(1987);* The Intellectuals and the Flag *(2006) and* The Bulldozer and the Big Tent: Blind Republicans, Lame Democrats, and the Recovery of the American Ideals *(2008) and the e-book* Occupy Nation: The Roots, the Spirit and the Promise of Occupy Wall Street *(2012). And then there are the hundreds of articles, columns and blogs he has written.*

On email, Gitlin is a man after my own heart; he emails back within hours at any time of the day or night. Emailing him from Australia, I was always surprised to see a return email from him pop into my inbox, when I knew it was past midnight in New York. His emails were always friendly and provided me with information about train timetables and directions. When he signed one of his emails 'looking forward to seeing you', I was excited. Gitlin enjoys the dynamic of the interview and I didn't want to disappoint him.

Originally I was going to catch the Amtrak train from Penn Station and meet him in the town of Hudson but his plans changed and instead, I was invited to Gitlin's apartment on Broadway. It is the kind of apartment that I could only ever dream about: beautiful, cultured; a little like a museum with artwork and sculptures. But it wasn't cold like a museum; Gitlin was very welcoming. There is something sleek and powerful about him. When we stood, staring out of the window at his neighbour's American flag, and Gitlin started discussing patriotism, I held my breath during each one of his pauses.

CA The first thing I noticed about your book, *The Intellectuals and The Flag* is that it is dedicated to your students. Do you think it is important for public intellectuals to teach and do you think you learn things from your students?

GITLIN Well, the second part is easier to answer. I learn what's in the moment. I learn what is alive to different generations. So, I don't learn from them in the sense that somebody may speak of learning a language. It is more a matter of being refreshed by angles that come to a subject. Or even styles of declining a subject, which hadn't occurred to me. It throws you for a loop in a healthy way to be questioned by someone who doesn't come to a subject with a pre-formed package of received ideas. So, in that sense, teaching is an enormous stimulant. And actually, I would say, at this point in my life, more so than ever before.

CA Really? Why do you think that?

GITLIN It has a lot to do with the fact that at Columbia, I am teaching undergraduates. Columbia is one of the few universities or liberal arts colleges in America that has a core curriculum. I teach a Great Books course. Every student at Columbia College takes it. It is taught in small sections with twenty-two students each. From the second year I started working here, I started teaching one of these sections of the course called Contemporary Civilization, which is basically a political theory, philosophy, religion, history course. It used to be called, informally, 'From Plato to NATO'. So, these are very smart students. Some of them are really quite stunning. There is something fundamental about this subject matter when students get interested in Kantian ethics or the reformation. Many of them are coming to it with a deep concern, as one should come to such subjects. This is not a casual business. In a way, it transcends the professional; these are life questions—these are questions of life philosophy they are asking. At the same time, I am also immersing myself in the fundamentals of thought that require close attention and I can't 'coast' on what I already know. I'm plunging back! When I started teaching this course, it was a matter of re-reading some texts that I hadn't read since college, myself. So now I'm brushing up against these enormities. This is enormously demanding; I am actually putting a lot more energy into teaching than I ever have before. And the students are very rewarding in all kinds of ways. It was not until I came here that I ever even contemplated that. That is a long-winded answer to your question. What was the first part of the question?

CA Do you think public intellectuals should teach?

GITLIN For me, it was never a choice. There was a period in my life where I tried to make a living as a freelance writer, but I couldn't do it. I think it all worked out, fortunately for me. The benefits are great and it turned out that I could maintain a pace of writing without any detriment. I think there are useful things a certain kind of writer could do without steady contact with students but I think there is a reason why many important writers in America have taught, alongside writing—and I don't think it has been simply for the money. E. L. Doctorow still teaches at NYU. Philip Roth, probably one of our most successful serious writers, for years taught a course, I think every semester, at least once a year. I don't think he needed the money. I think he wanted to do it for stimulus. Even teachers should have some time off from it! I wouldn't say someone should be ruled out of the 'exclusive club' of intellectuals if they don't teach; but I do think there is a benefit to it.

CA What do you think are the responsibilities of the public intellectual to himself and to the public?

GITLIN I think one is obliged to ask difficult questions; questions that are difficult for one's public. I think one is obliged to prod and poke and edge them off the perches of what they take for granted. Often they will howl, 'Here comes the hypodermic needle, I don't really want this shot.' I've seen a good deal of that in my career and that's alright. However impassioned or opinionated one is and ought to be, I suppose, one is obliged not to be a silent team member or cheerleader. The risk of doing this sort of thing is that you become a propagandist for a cause. It is curious, I'd say in the last twenty years or so of my work, I can't imagine being any more impassioned than I have been. Neither would I want to have been more slovenly; more of a booster. I have no interest in being a booster. Being controversial on one side is something people need—even partisans need—whether they know it or not. That is an obligation. I have often felt dismayed and indignant at the sight of people who purport to be serious intellectuals who are in the business of just currying favour with their public. You don't do it to make friends.

CA What do you consider to be your style of teaching?

GITLIN I do very different kinds of teaching. I was speaking a few minutes ago about my undergrad. teaching. But I also teach in a PhD programme and I teach Masters level students in journalism. Most is at the level of undergraduate teaching or the PhD level teaching and it is quite different. PhD teaching is obviously at a level of specialty and professionalism whereas undergraduate teaching is more exploratory. I suppose a common element is that I tend toward a Socratic approach. When you are introducing a text you want to have a feel for the text; you want to give its due to a writer—even if it's a writer who you, yourself, think is wrong. As I said before, one doesn't want to be a propagandist in the classroom either, least of all. So in that sense there is this common element. When I am teaching Plato, I don't want to take cheap shots at Plato. When I am teaching the Koran or Martin Luther, I want to take students into the territory of considering 'what it would be like to be there?' The same thing would be true of teaching a cultural history or Habermas or anyone I might be teaching in a graduate seminar. I am very much partial to teaching small classes; teaching seminars. When I was at Berkeley, which is where I was for sixteen years, every year I taught large lecture classes—usually about 100–150 students and sometimes as many as 400 students—and I didn't not like it. I like lecturing occasionally, but to me it is a lower level of experience and I much prefer the small setting. I do, sometimes, promote—in a persnickety and Socratic way—for the sake of argument, a position that isn't mine. I do this just to see where I can go with it. In the undergraduate class, more than the graduate class, I will lecture, in a sense—that is, I will come in with notes and there will be some points I want to bring forward—but I still try to stay available for meanderings. As long as I know the fundamentals of play, I don't have an agenda. I do tell anecdotes but I don't think I do it routinely.

CA I read that you write during term time and I wondered how you manage with the demands of teaching and administration.

GITLIN I do, although not as much as I do during the summer. Something evolved in me—when I was young, I was a night person and I was worthless in the morning. In fact, when I was in college I couldn't really get up for morning classes, so I slept through them when I enrolled in them. Sometimes I would fall asleep in class, sometimes after staying up all night. Somewhere along the line I became a morning person. It was probably when I was writing in the sixties or maybe even earlier than that. I could do a day's work of writing before class. I try to teach classes no earlier than 11 in the morning. So, unless I have meetings, or something—which is uncommon—I can actually do a reasonable amount of work before I go off to teach. So that is how I do it. I tend to assign myself quotas of words. It is a lot easier in the age of the word count on computers but I was doing it even before computers. It depends on what kind of writing I am doing, but I keep count, I keep track and I pat myself on the back for surpassing my quoting and chastise myself for not. I can actually have a very full day that involves writing and teaching. Obviously during the summer and breaks I get more written but I can keep up something during term time.

CA You were a student radical in the '60s. Do you think your students are anywhere near as political as students were in the sixties and is it a good thing or a bad thing?

GITLIN Graduate students in the social sciences and humanities tend to be left wing, in some fashion or other. Few of them are activists, at least while they are in the PhD programme—but some of them are. When I was a graduate student, I was president of SDS [Students for a Democratic Society], it's not like that now. I've had a few undergraduates who are political activists. It is the luck of the draw. Students who take CC [Contemporary Civilisation] don't get to choose their instructor. So it has been an accident that I have actually had some of the most activist students. But they are exceptional; I would say there are five to ten per cent who are activists. It is a different time. They are representative of this moment. Maybe I don't always know which ones are activists—but I think after a few weeks they generally make themselves known to me. You can't necessarily tell by how they operate in class. At a certain point they discover something about my background. I generally don't make much of it, I might mention it in passing by way of introducing myself—that I was a student radical in the sixties. They tend to seek me out.

CA How important is the media's role in the public intellectual's life?

GITLIN The media is in the air we are breathing and, truly, they matter in all kinds of ways. If you were a political operative in the late eighteenth or early nineteenth century Britain and you didn't have any contact with factories, then surely you would have consigned yourself to some kind of marginality and intellectual triviality, as well. So, you have to be in contact with the cultural centres of your time. By the same token, if you want to either be an educator or political agitator—and there is obviously an overlap between them—and you cut yourself off from the primary instruments of cultural transmission and ritual, you are amputating your possibilities. I say this with enormous suspicion and apprehension because the media are also muck and junk heaps. So, it is a treacherous business and one has to be careful about how one approaches media. There are intellectuals I admire like David Riesman, who wouldn't have anything to do with television. I respect that. I think it is harder to do today if you are trying to do the sort of thing he was trying to do. I am mindful, amused, horrified and apprehensive about the media world and what happens when you step through it in a gauche way.

CA What do you think about postmodernism and language? How important is writing style to the public intellectual? Some French theorists are/were writing English as a second language and many people try to ape this mystifying style.

GITLIN Yes, theory as a second language! Style is a sine qua non of clarity—and not just clarity of communication, but clarity of thought. I knew Foucault when he was at Berkeley. He spent much of his last few years at Berkeley. He was extremely lucid in English. To be a substantial French intellectual, one has to commit a certain level of bullshit. Foucault admitted it and Pierre Bourdieu admitted it. It is quite apparent. These are people who were capable of being extremely and methodically clear and they performed pirouettes and spun arabesques because it was expected of them. They knew the game. It is one thing to spin the pirouettes if it is the stylistic form of one's moment. If one were a composer in a certain era one had to learn to write fugues. If you were a poet in a certain moment—except with the great pioneers of style—you had to learn to write sonnets. You learn to master the forms of the moment. Those who would emulate Foucault have tried to place themselves in that tradition but it is rather laughable. Foucault, when he was functioning as a public person, whether as a lecturer in English—I mean I don't know what his lectures were like in French, I never heard him give a lecture in French, but I have read some of them in French—they are actually more lucid than the writing. Certainly, when he was functioning as a political activist he was not as Delphic, let's say, as he was in written prose.

This is all so interesting and peculiar. I have spent some time in France. Foucault doesn't have the kind of significance that he does for English speaking people, in France. He is one of many. Derrida, likewise, was not such a formidable figure. There are pleasures in any developed style and as I understand the appeal of the style, I think that also—for personal or public impulse—this is more a trap than a benefit. To style oneself a connoisseur of a style that is artificial in the first place, and then to be artificial at two removes from lucidity is, I think, pathetic and laughable. There is nothing more tedious than somebody straining to produce this kind of thing. When I was at Berkeley, I was sometimes on the admissions committee for the graduate programme in sociology and at a certain point I became aware that we would get theory minded applicants trying to 'do' Foucault. They would send in these essays which were their versions of Foucault and sometimes—usually, against my protest—we would admit them. None of them finished. Some of them were psychotic. It was a style that was comfortable for people at a considerable remove from 'reality', not just in a conventional sense. The style of Foucault appealed to people who saw speech and style as performance—and performance of the self-contained sort. I was once a mathematician and I understand the pleasures of the self-enclosed, axiomatic system. This has some of the same contours—although, mathematics has the beauty and this doesn't. This is ugly writing and, for the most part, ugly thinking.

CA My fiancé is an academic in American history in Australia and he brings students to America every year on a study tour. One of the things they always comment on is the number of American flags flying and the patriotism. Do you think that makes Americans more unquestioning of their government and therefore, more likely to go off and fight?

GITLIN The French know the words to their anthem, but they don't fly their flag everywhere. Ségoléne Royal actually proposed it during the presidential campaign and I think he was mocked for it. I don't know if I can answer the question. I would say that the automatic flying of the flag tends to co-exist with servility towards government policy, which is disturbing. I distinguish between symbolic patriotism and substantial patriotism. I still would sustain that distinction. It may well be true that—I don't know—I guess here I want to go social science-y on it. I don't know of anyone who has ever studied what meanings people associate with the flag. Let me show you something. [He takes me over to the window]. Since I moved into this building …

CA Have you been here long?

GITLIN Just four years! There is somebody flying a flag here.

CA It's pretty big.

GITLIN It is pretty big and it has been there for at least four years. Whether it was there before September 11, I have no idea. What should we assume about that? I really don't know. This is one of the more liberal, in an American sense, areas in America—the Upper West Side of Manhattan. This is a left wing haven. Is that guy flying the flag a Bush supporter? I don't know. If you drove around in upstate New York, where I have my summer place, you see a lot of flags flying. Around July 4, you see more of them, but some people are flying them all year round. Is it statistically the case that they are more likely to be Bush supporters, Republicans? I don't know. It may well be true. It has all kinds of meanings. In areas like that, which are more economically depressed, the affirmation that the nation is yours is a kind of assertion of identity, which matters to people. This is the same as in Britain—or maybe in Australia, I don't know—where people feel affiliated or connected to mass history is an affirmation of bravado or dignity—some sort of declaration of 'who I am.' The idea that I belong to something which transcends my boundaries, my ego ... It wouldn't surprise me if I saw an association statistically between the display of the flag and a certain adherence to government policy or government style at a given moment. But it wouldn't entirely amaze me if that correlation were weak—I just don't know!

'If you don't want to take risks, then you have to be silent'

Howard Zinn

I was sad to read that Howard Zinn died in January 2010. After reading A People's History of the United States *in my first year of studying history at university, I was devoted to him and to reading his books. He loved the working person; he gave them a voice when every other history book I had read prioritised the elite. I had always loved the story of the way in which fate intervened in Zinn's life. Perhaps he would have lived out his years a shipbuilder if not for his role as a bombardier in World War II and the GI Bill. He went to college under the GI Bill, studying history at New York University and then undertaking an MA and PhD at Columbia. However, it is clear that his experiences in the war led him to be a staunch participant in the anti-war movement.*

Zinn worked at Spelman College in Atlanta, Georgia in 1956. It was a black women's college and it was here that he taught, among others, Alice Walker. When he encouraged the women at this college to be active politically, rather than focusing on becoming 'ladies', he was fired for insubordination. Zinn then moved to Boston University in 1964 where he worked as a professor in political science until he retired in 1988.

It was snowing on the day I went to Zinn's house. He lived in Auberndale, MA in a huge red, shingle-topped house. He ushered me in when I rang the doorbell and we sat in a tastefully decorated living room full of beautiful ornaments. The first things I noticed about Zinn were how slim and fit he was and how his eyes smiled when I asked him a question. There was a real mischievousness about him, a glint in his eye; a total animation of his face when he told a story. He could have been an actor; it was not surprising that he became a playwright because his understanding of the way in which theatre can elicit an emotional response to a series of events or a particular historical period was far-reaching. I loved how quick he was to laugh and how he made me feel comfortable in his home. It's no wonder his students loved him; he had a wonderful way of listening intently and responding graciously to everything he was asked. In the end, he reminded me of his friend, Noam Chomsky, but somehow a more modest and calmer version of Chomsky. Zinn loved his life. He loved teaching. He loved writing. He loved devoting himself to a political campaign. He loved being invited to give speeches all over the world. So Zinn was doing what he loved when he died, prior to giving a speech at The Santa Monica Museum of Art, aptly titled, 'The People Speak'. I feel honoured to have interviewed him and to have heard him speak.

CA What do you think are the responsibilities of the public intellectual to himself and to the public?

ZINN To respect what you do, and in order to respect, you have to feel that you are doing more than being an ordinary, traditional academic. I think you have a responsibility to yourself to live the most fruitful life that you can, a life that will make you feel that you are doing something for society and not something just to satisfy your own personal ambition. A responsibility to society is a responsibility that not only intellectuals should have—it is a responsibility that every human being should have. The difference is that intellectuals have a special position in society, which enables them to do things that many people are not in a position to do—these are people whose jobs occupy their lives; people whose lives are fraught with all sorts of problems; who don't have the time, the tools, the wherewithal to make a contribution. The intellectual has certain qualities: special tools; education; time; and the possibility of reaching numbers of people, which an ordinary person cannot do. The intellectual has the capacity to fulfil that responsibility to society and a special duty to do so because the intellectual lives a privileged life [gestures to the opulence around him]. The intellectual is lucky. The intellectual may complain—they often do—but the intellectual lives a life of relative ease compared to the rest of the world—and I'm not even talking about the third world, I am talking about people in an advanced industrial prosperous country like the United States. But most people in the United States are not in a position to enjoy life in the way that an intellectual can because of the demands made of them just for survival. So I think the intellectual has a special responsibility to use his/her special qualities, special time, special position to do something for the world.

CA As a public intellectual you may come up against people who heartily disagree with you and your ideas. Is that difficult?

ZINN That is the risk you must take. If you don't want to take risks then you have to be silent. As soon as you speak up or express a point of view, you are taking a risk that there will be people who disagree with you. And, in fact, there is something positive about that because it means that you are throwing out your argument into a contentious world—a world in which people have different points of view. You are adding your point of view to one side of the argument. You are playing a part in the ongoing debate, instead of standing inside and withdrawing from it. If you are an intellectual who speaks out then you must accept it, enjoy it, even relish it, make the most of it. In fact, you sharpen your own intellectual tools and your own political ideas by listening to the opposition. So the opposing viewpoints are not simply things that you must be on guard against and figure out how you can defeat. The oppositional arguments are things which the intellectual must listen to and then may be forced to reconsider his or her position or to modify that position. So there is a usefulness to this opposition. Intellectuals who don't want any opposition should stay out of the public arena.

CA You said that universities aren't the only place for public intellectuals, but can you discuss the benefits and problems with being allied to a university and being a public intellectual?

ZINN The benefit of being attached to a university is that you have an immediate listening audience. You have students, young people, the upcoming generation—a very important generation—people who you are in contact with, whom you get to know, who presumably respect your opinions, who will listen to the suggestions you make about what they read. So this is an enormous advantage as opposed to an intellectual who lives a kind of cloistered life and must struggle to go out and reach people. So if you are in the university, you have this special audience right at hand, and then of course a certain amount of economic security which a freelance intellectual has great difficulty coming by. It is very hard to be an intellectual not attached to a university because how are you going to make a living? If you are a writer or a poet you are in a market-driven society which doesn't cherish poets and writers. And so the university gives you that time, freedom and economic security. On the other hand, the university can hamper you. It can hamper you by the constraints that the academic world places on an intellectual who has very strong political opinions. Generally, universities—and by this I mean university administrations, which not only include top administrators, trustees, regents, presidents, deans and so on but also the chair of your department and the colleagues in your department—very often they may try to limit what you do in public and limit what you do politically. Very often the traditional members of a university community, the administrators, but also faculty, are made nervous by contact with the political conflicts that swirl all around the university. So that is a handicap that the intellectual in the university had to guard against and be prepared to resist.

CA How do you juggle the demands of teaching and administration with research and writing? Are they in any way reciprocal?

ZINN It helps if you can in some way link what you do in the classroom with what you do outside. It is easier for somebody who teaches politics, history, sociology. It's harder for someone who teaches physics or organic chemistry, although with a little ingenuity, they can do it. Certainly teachers of literature very devilishly choose pieces of literature that reflect their values! And, in fact, I have used pieces of literature in my courses because I thought they were so useful. So, although your time is limited, university teaching puts great demands on your time. But that is if you are a conscientious teacher, if you are not, then university is a wonderful place to goof off! But if you are a conscientious teacher, you are working at your teaching all the time and so it does limit the amount of time you have for outside political activity. The great advantage of having one foot in each sphere is that each can augment and enrich the other. Your scholarly work, your academic work, can be very useful and help a great deal in dealing with problems of a political movement that you are attached to. Political movements need facts, they need research, they need analysis. Well, here you are, you are in a position to do that and to do work which will serve you in both spheres. There is an advantage to your political activity by being in the classroom, and there is an advantage to your teaching by being out in the world because you can bring into the classroom the experiences that an ivory tower dweller will not have. And not only that; your teaching will have much more meaning to the students if they know that it comes out of life experience, which is not just based on books. So trying to be in both spheres creates difficulties, but it is also very valuable when this kind of cross fertilisation takes place.

CA Can you tell me a bit about your style of teaching?

ZINN I use film, documentary film, sometimes even feature films to great advantage in the classroom. When I was teaching about Vietnam I used this film, *Hearts and Minds*. It is very powerful. I used a film called *Attica,* which is about the Attica prison uprising in the United States in 1971 and suppressed brutally by the governor of New York state. I used a Marlon Brando movie called *Burn*, probably the least known of all Brando movies, because it was not publicised due to the fact that it was a revolutionary movie. It was about a slave revolt in a Portuguese colony in the nineteenth century; an anti-imperialist movie. It is the one Marlon Brando movie that was hidden from sight. It was even withdrawn from circulation for a number of years. I used a number of movies in my classes because they could accomplish things that I could not. For example, what could be said about the Vietnam War by that movie—not only the amount of information, but what it captures of the emotional intensity—is something I could not convey in the same effective way. I would very often play recordings of Malcolm X to my class and scare the hell out of them—all of these white people, you see. But it could give them a sense of the rage in black people that I could not give them myself.

I have never used slides. When I speak now—since I stopped teaching I have been doing a lot of speaking—they always ask me if I want any of the new visual technologies, slides. I say, 'No'. I don't think I would know how to use it and I prefer not to. I tried in my classes to have as much interchange with students as possible and to give them as much time as possible as they need to respond to me. I tried to create an atmosphere in which students felt free to disagree with me, didn't have to worry about getting bad grades.

CA One of the things you have said is that to be a good teacher you have to share your political views, you have to be honest about your beliefs. How important is it to share what you believe in with your class?

ZINN Very often the reason given for not sharing your opinion is that it can be intimidating to the students. Sure, that is a possibility and therefore you have to make it clear that while you are expressing your opinions very strongly, you understand that yours may not be right. You have to acknowledge that students have their own opinions; that there are conflicting views. One of the ways of doing this is by never punishing anybody with a bad grade because of their opinions. Word gets around about teachers who are punishing that way and also about teachers who are tolerant that way. I think one reason it is important to share your views with students, is not because you are trying to influence students, but because you are trying to influence the *way* they think. You are not trying to command what they think, but at least introduce them to ideas that they may not have. One of the reasons for doing this is that it says something to the student about not withholding your ideas no matter what profession you are in.

These students are not all going to be teachers. Some of them will be, some of them will be in the business world, and so on and so forth. But I think what you are saying to them is, 'Look, whatever walk of life you are in you should not be constrained by the barriers that are set up by the idea that as a professional you should keep your political opinions to yourself.' I saw a doctor last week for a medical exam. I hadn't even introduced myself but he recognised my name. He said to me, 'Didn't you give a talk at a high school and there was some controversy about it?' And I said, 'Yeah!' He said, 'I'm not political, but Bush and Cheney, they have to go!'

CA You were placed on a list of America's most dangerous public intellectuals by Horowicz. Are you dangerous?

ZINN I was honoured to be on the list. Dangerous? I hope so. I wish I were dangerous. I guess anybody with dissident ideas is slightly dangerous and none of us is that dangerous. Our hope is that if you put one million slightly dangerous people together that it will create enormous danger.

CA You have a wonderful writing style; a great fluency. What do you think about postmodernist writing style?

ZINN It is a problem. I am very impatient with mystification, with pretentious language and a pretty closed circle of people who are the only ones who understand what is being said. One of the important aspects of being a public intellectual is that the public must know what you are saying; must be able to understand what you are saying. This is true in a classroom where you can't try to impress students. Certainly with writing, the academic world hones people's natural writing ability. It seems the higher up you go, the worse the language gets. A PhD student will write in this manner, and why is that? The student has gotten the message that if you really want to be considered an important academic and a real scholar you must use this kind of language. Of course, to me that is an anathema. Clear, concise communication is the most important thing.

CA You have written about how the GI bill gave you the chance to go to college. With the inequalities in education, do working class students have a chance to be a part of the intelligentsia or academia?

ZINN There is more pressure on working class students. They come from poor families, they are barely making their way through the academic world. There is great pressure on them to get jobs and income and so it is harder for them. On the other hand, if they do decide that they must somehow enter the fray—with all these difficulties—they are in a better position to educate the people. Because they are class conscious and can infuse that class consciousness into others and there is a kind of solidity to their background that makes what they say about the world more credible. Somebody told me a few years ago that they were writing a book researching people who teach at universities; academics, that come from working class backgrounds—that is an interesting thing to do.

CA If you come from a working class background and get into the university, can you still be a spokesperson for the working classes?

ZINN It is a little more difficult than if you came into the classroom still wearing the miner's helmet, your hands greasy, saying: 'I have just come out of the mines, kids, let me talk to you!' And here you are, a college professor, wearing a suit. But I think it is possible. It is harder, but it is possible to hold on to your background and it depends on you as a person. There are many people in the academic world who come from working class backgrounds who put it behind them—who want to put it behind them—who don't want anything to do with that. But on the other hand, if you come from such a background and you are not renouncing it and you want to maintain that connection, then it is in you and you can impart to the students that even though now you are middle class, your parents were working class—maybe even you were working class until you were eighteen years old. But I think it is possible to impart to your students that feeling of being part of the working class that you once had.

CA Are public intellectuals reduced to only ever commenting on current public policy with little chance to effect its change?

ZINN The effect that you have on government policy will always be indirect. You try to make what you say, write and teach as directly connected with present policy as possible. You may be teaching eighteenth century literature and there is a gap or chasm between teaching and policy. This piece of literature is laden with social significance but it is a far cry from immediate public policy. You face this tricky dilemma. You don't want to politicise everything in a very crass way and therefore not pay sufficient attention to that particular period/event/literature; not distort its essence by insisting that it must have some immediate connection to what is going on today. At the same time, I think there are times where you can leave it to the students and you should leave it to them to make the connections themselves. We don't have to make the connection. If they are reading Thomas Hardy and something is obviously being said about marriage and the freedom of individuals, you don't have to spell out in relation to what is happening today. It should be evident. So you very often can leave it to students to make that connect with present policy.

Anything that public intellectuals do is only going to have an indirect effect. It is very rare that you get the opportunity to do something directly. The things that you do outside the classroom will have more direct impact outside of the classroom, like sitting in the senator's office and demanding the senator vote a certain way in a certain bill. What you are doing in a classroom is creating a mindset for the student which might lead that student tomorrow to go and sit in the senator's office.

CA I want to come back to fiction. How important is fiction in capturing a particular moment in history?

ZINN As you probably know I have used fiction in my classes and I have used it precisely because I thought that a novel or a play or poem can bring an idea or the history of an epic home to a student, more vividly with an intensity that you rarely find in non-fiction. Therefore, you can take an idea presented in non-fiction and when compared to the same idea presented in fiction, it will have far less emotional impact. I think I have used the example of the lecture on the 1930s in the United States and explained how terrible it was with people lined up in the streets for food baskets and so on and so forth. Or you could have them read *The Grapes of Wrath* and they will viscerally understand what it was like to live in such hard times.

CA You have written a play. I am fascinated that you write analytically and creatively. Do you find one harder than the other?

ZINN Creative writing is more difficult. Think of Henry James and Kurt Vonnegut who had hard times writing plays. I'm telling you all of this to explain why it's harder to write a play. It *is* harder to write a play. I can write a non-fiction book in a year, it takes me years to put all the elements together for a play. It requires more imagination. I mean, how much imagination do you need to write a regular history book? It's harder but more rewarding.

CA Do you enjoy seeing your play performed?

ZINN I don't like to admit how much I enjoy seeing my play on stage. But of course I do! It's exciting. It is as if a writer sat himself down in front of someone who was reading his book and watched his facial expressions and took pleasure out of it. It is fun to see your work on stage. The great thing that I discovered about writing for theatre is that you now are part of a collective enterprise. As a writer you are isolated and as a playwright your play is immediately taken over by a director and stage designer and a cast—the actors—and you become an ensemble and little affinity group of people. And it is a great feeling. In the theatre people hug one another. The members of my department don't hug one another!

CA Which writers do you admire, both fiction and non-fiction?

ZINN Dickens, Tolstoy and in the United States, Steinbeck and Upton Sinclair and Sinclair Lewis, Melville, and for non-fiction Bertrand Russell for his clarity of language. Philosophers are very often so mystical and Bertrand Russell and John Dewey were two philosophers who wrote with clarity. William James did too. Noam Chomsky, who doesn't always write simply, although in his interviews where there is no opportunity for footnotes he is much more approachable. I mentioned of course that Vonnegut is one of my favourite novelists and Heller and Catch 22. Arthur Miller as a playwright is always a model for me.

'Who Drank the Hemlock?' *Noam Chomsky*

I interviewed Noam Chomsky on my honeymoon, two days after I got married in Boston. It's a good thing I married a history professor who understood the significance of taking the opportunity to interview Professor Chomsky at Massachusetts Institute of Technology, (MIT). My new husband even came with me and idled around the campus while I went up to Professor Chomsky's office, pretending not to be jealous that I was meeting one of his heroes. In fact, he made me promise to ask Chomsky about unions, as my husband is a labor historian.

The name 'Chomsky' is magic. People listen when you invoke his name, wanting to know what he was like; if I was overwhelmed by his intellect; if he was intimidating.

I had been told to go to the eighth floor of the State Building in Vassar Street at MIT, in the Dreyfoos Tower. I was one hour early—you don't keep someone like Chomsky waiting. I sat for a while in the MIT cafeteria. My hands were so sweaty that the pages of my notebook were wavy and crinkled. Nerd pride surrounded me. Students whose pants were just that little bit too short, stereotypical thick-rimmed glasses were everywhere and so I bought a t-shirt that said Cutie p and wished I had a science degree. I would have liked to go to MIT. There is something cool about the geometric shapes and primary colours, not to mention all the research that has come out of MIT. I tried to distract myself by reading plaques dedicated to famous alumni on the walls.

When I made my way up to Chomsky's office I was told to sit and wait outside, as he was still busy with a video conference. He strolled past me, casually dressed, somehow smaller in frame than I imagined, for an intellectual giant. He asked me to give him a moment and then invited me into his office. Books were piled everywhere, and I was glad, I wouldn't have had his office any other way; it was exactly as I had pictured it. Piles of books rose like stalagmites from every available space. He had a cup, I assume it was coffee, which he moved around the desk as we spoke. I fleetingly thought about how much money I could get for that cup on eBay. I mean, here I was, sitting opposite the most famous academic, dissident public intellectual, probably the most intelligent man in the world.

Was I overwhelmed by his intellect? Yes. Was he intimidating? Only because of his intellect and integrity. What was he like? He was gentle and very softly spoken. In fact he said that his voice didn't often record well and listening back to the interview, his voice often drops to a whisper. But it is his eyes that I remember most. They sparkled when I asked a question. The joy of answering questions about things for which he felt some kind of passion was obvious from the twinkle in his velvet eyes.

CA What are the responsibilities of the public intellectual both to him/herself and the public?

CHOMSKY Well, that is really two questions; one is what they are and the second is what they should be. What they are, is what Hans Morgenthau, the founder of realist international relations theory, said: conformist subservients to those in power. That is basically correct throughout history. You can trace this back to the bible or classical Greece. So who drank the hemlock? In Athens, it wasn't somebody who was praising the gods, it was someone who was corrupting the youth. In the bible there are people who we would call intellectuals—they're called prophets but that's just a bad translation due to the obscurity of the word—but they are what we call intellectuals. However, the prophets were criticising the acts of the evil kings—they were carrying out political analysis and were calling for mercy and justice for the suffering people. That is what we would argue an intellectual should do, but how were they treated? They were driven into the desert and imprisoned and were called haters of Israel. They were called anti-Semites.

There were intellectuals who were treated very well. They were the ones who, centuries later in the gospels, were called the false prophets. They were the flatterers of the court, the conformists, those committed to conformist subservience to those in power. They were the ones who were well treated, praised and lauded and so on—and so it goes in history. I mean you can find some exceptions, but not many. If you look through history you will find that it is the conformist intellectuals who are respected and honoured. In the old Soviet Union, it's the commissars and not the dissidents who are respected; dissidents could be praised in the west but not in the Soviet Union. Of course, dissidents in the United States, aren't sent to the gulag. We have other ways in the west for marginalising and silencing the voices that aren't liked. Orwell wrote about that in his introduction to *Animal Farm*. He said, in free countries like in England, unpopular views can be suppressed without the use of force. He goes on to talk about this, but his voice was suppressed; his introduction wasn't published.

CA Can you discuss the benefits and the drawbacks of a public intellectual working in a university as there has been some debate about whether a public intellectual should be allied to a university or not.

CHOMSKY Should Marx not have worked in the British museum? The British museum is the symbol of empire, it stole everything from all around the world—so should Marx have refused to use the resources from the British museum? It is an extremely irrational attitude and it is also a deeply immoral one. I mean we should be concerned about what people do, not where they are working or who is paying them. We have had this debate around here for the past 60 years for obvious reasons. MIT is theoretically a private university, but basically a government university. Until the 1970s it was close to one hundred percent supported by the pentagon. But did that mean that we should not have organised resistance against the Vietnam War in a lab which was one hundred percent supported by the three armed services?

CA Is it hard though to stay true to your roots when you are in a privileged environment? How do you stay connected to the people?

CHOMSKY Just take a look at the few dissidents scattered around. A great many of them are pretty privileged Americans, because they have opportunities. Privilege confers opportunity. People can use it to be subservient to those in power if they want to, but they have other options. So take MIT again. In the 1960s when I was actively involved in resistance and in and out of jail—facing all sorts of charges—there was no reaction from the university or the Pentagon. And there is good reason for that, which a lot of people don't know—including most economists. We don't have a free market economy; nothing like it. We have an economy that relies very heavily on state sectors. MIT is kind of like the funnel into which the population pours money, thinking that it is for defence or something. Of course it isn't, and out of the funnel comes high technology which can be handed over to private corporations for profit; that's the economy. That's where you get computers, the internet, telecommunications, biotechnology—run through the list. They are mostly publicly subsidised through institutions like this, under one or another pretext, for a long time. However, the pretext is generally the same, to an extent. It is basically creating the economy of the future. The Pentagon understands that, even if the Economics department doesn't. Because they don't care if you want to rip into the government, you've already done your work.

But then you have to ask the real question: what is the consequence of the work that you do? And if you are working on biological warfare with a grant from the NIH, it's no better than if you're working on biological warfare with a grant from the Pentagon. The source of the funding is essentially irrelevant, unless the source of the funding controls what you do. If that is the case, then simple questions of honesty arise. But other than that, the universities are probably the freest institutions in the country—so why not work there? Why not have a student movement at a place where students and young people can actually do something, instead of being controlled by their parents or working in a job, fifty hours a week, and not being able to put food on the table? They are lucky here, they are privileged, they are free; they should use the opportunity. To tell them to leave their freedom and opportunity is irrational and immoral. There are pressures—I understand the point of view, in fact I have friends who hold the same views and I have argued with them about this. I understand their views. I just think it is a mistake.

CA I wanted you to discuss the impact of teaching and writing on each other. Do you see one as informing the other?

CHOMSKY Most of my writing is, in fact, something that came out of class talks and class discussions. I just spent an hour on a video conference with Pakistan where they asked me to give a talk on a topic that I hadn't expected. It just so happens that I have to write an article on a similar topic and I think what I will do—if I can remember what I said—is take what I said and use it for the article. Professional work, everything I have written, has come out of class.

CA How important do you think it is to share your political views with your students?

CHOMSKY I'm very scrupulous about that; I never do. I mean, they bring it up, but I don't like to talk to captive audiences. It is one of the reasons why I don't give the commencement speeches. I'm constantly asked to do commencement speeches, and I used to do them years ago, but I don't do them now. The reason is straightforward; the audience is not coming to hear my political views. I mean if I give a talk, I can talk about my political views. A couple of days ago I gave a talk in one of the towns around here. I was able to say whatever I wanted, because people came and wanted to hear what I had to say. But when you do a commencement speech, you are talking to the parents of students, and they don't want to hear what I have to say—so what right do I have to force them to listen? And it is the same when you are talking to students—I do sometimes offer my views, but on my own time, not in class time. I taught undergraduate courses on political and social issues for about twenty-five years. I did discuss my thoughts in those courses, because the students were coming to hear it. However, if I am giving a linguistics seminar, I might make a joke, but that is all.

CA Do you think public intellectuals can shape government policy or are you always on the back foot having to discuss the policy that is already out there rather than shape the vision?

CHOMSKY Again, we have to ask which public intellectuals. If you are talking about the ones who can publish in the press and the journals and who are respected and so on—then yes, they can shape and in fact design public policy. They can try to manipulate the public into accepting it, as this is a part of their role. If you are talking about dissident intellectuals, the only way they can shape government policy is by addressing the population and the population can then, one way or another, affect public policy. Even in totalitarian states they have to pay some attention to public intellectuals, and then in freer societies it can have a substantial role. But, it is only through such indirect means as that.

CA How do dissident public intellectuals get their ideas across if the media is filtering everything they say? I have read that you have written letters to newspapers and journals that haven't been published.

CHOMSKY I rarely write letters, I know that they won't publish them. I do it out of curiosity sometimes, to see how low they can sink. Like if the *Wall Street Journal* or the *New York Times* or somebody publishes pure lies and slander, will they let me respond? That is where my curiosity lies. If I look back over fifty years, there are times when I have had access to the media and that is because they are capable of misunderstanding what I am saying. This has been at very specific times, like towards the end of the Vietnam War. The intellectuals, the business community, turned against the war after the defence of 1968. Once the business conglomerate took a stand, that opened up lots of things in the corporate media. And at that point, it was possible for people like me to write and publish in the public media, giving a principled critique of the war and saying that it is wrong, not because it is costing too much or because it is failing, but because it's aggression. This was only possible because it could be misunderstood as joining the mainstream public intellectuals in their unprincipled critique of the war.

Their critique of the war was approximately like it's been in Australia. It's like the Nazi generals after Stalingrad who could say to Hitler that we should never have opened a two front war; it was stupid. We should have taken out Britain first, or something. That is the standard critique of the Vietnam War at the moment. It's the same with Iraq. Take a look at the discussions today. It is all about whether we can win, and if it is costing too much money. Sometimes it is overly dramatic. In the *New York Times* magazine Michael Gordon discussed the war and the election and he used the various options that the United States had in Iraq; he put the candidates, the government officials, military people, liberal critics and the full range in a potentially serious article. There is only one voice missing and that is the Iraqis' voice. It is not that they don't know what the Iraqis think, they do. In fact, a spectacular report came out recently from the Pentagon. The Pentagon carries out regular inquiries into Iraqi opinion, probably the Nazis did the same. If you want to control or dominate a population, you have to know what they think. Well, they released a report, which was very enthusiastic. They said there is good news, most people think that with sectarian violence and ethnic conflict the Iraqis will never get together—but we have discovered from our study that Iraqis really have shared beliefs. From all over the country and from all walks of life they agree on important trends. And this is good news. So what are the shared beliefs? It turns out the shared beliefs are that the United States is to blame for all the atrocities that have taken place and that it should get out and then maybe they could have national reconciliation. That is what the Iraqis think, but that doesn't enter the discussion.

The British diplomatic historian named Mark Curtis, who is a serious public intellectual—so he can't be quoted or referred to—has written a book on Britain's horrendous crimes, often very candidly. He is very good but he has a book called *Unpeople*. Meaning, just 'people', but not us guys with the brains and the guns—the general population. So the Iraqis are unpeopled; their voice doesn't matter. Just like the voice of Americans doesn't matter either, because that's another voice that gets dismissed—unpeople.

And that is the role of public intellectuals to make sure that people and unpeople are never heard and that the only thing that is heard is the voice of those with power and privilege. Of course, they think of themselves as very critical and dissident. So Anthony Lewis, who I have quoted, will be outraged to hear that I think that he was kind of like a Nazi after Stalingrad. But is it true? Yes, it is true.

CA Communication is a really important part of connecting with the public and I wanted to ask you about post-modernism and what you think about postmodernism and its affect on writing and analysis.

CHOMSKY Postmodernism is a very useful invention to keep intellectuals in their preferred status of conformist subservients to those in power. It is mostly unintelligible gibberish. I look at it, but mostly out of curiosity. It falls into two categories as far as I can see: unintelligible and truism. The truism is said in very inflated rhetoric, polysyllables and so on. What it turns out to be, is a way for intellectuals to be more radical than thou, but do nothing except talk to each other in academic seminars and not get involved with the general public in real activism. That is very attractive, it is a lot of fun to sit around having conversations with one another as Richard Rorty put it, and it is really wonderful to want to get involved in the nitty gritty of organising workers or illegal immigrants. But it is a cocoon, almost impenetrable, impossible to understand what they are talking about.

CA Camille Paglia was saying to me that French theorists like Barthes and Foucault were writing English as a second language and that it is ridiculous; American (and Australian) theorists trying to ape this language.

CHOMSKY You should read it in French, it's much worse. Have you read Jean Bricmont, the Belgian physicist and Alan Sokel's, American physicist, *Intellectual Impostures*? They went through what leading French intellectuals had written about science, and it was so outlandish, you can't believe that human beings who went to junior high school could write things like that. But when you write it in very inflated rhetoric with codicils and pomposity and so on, people take it seriously.

There is one of these post-modern French guys, Latour, who has a background in Science. He wrote an article in response to the discovery that one of the Pharaohs had died of tuberculosis. Latour wrote a very cynical article about this thing and how ridiculous it was to think that this Pharaoh had died of tuberculosis because tuberculosis was only discovered in the nineteenth century. And we all know that there is no truth, there is only social construction, so isn't it silly they claimed he died of tuberculosis?

You think that people are parodying themselves. My own personal view, but I can't prove it, is that he was trying to see how ridiculous he could be and still be taken seriously by Bricmont. Apparently, the only thing he could think of was to close down his Institute—it made font page news. It is a very strange culture. I should say that when that stuff is picked up by intellectuals in Australia or the United States, it doesn't matter much, they just play their games. But where it is really lethal is in the third world because third world intellectuals tend to stand in a certain awe of western culture, especially Paris. I see, all over the third world, intellectuals aping the latest Paris nonsense and it is serious there, because the popular movements really need great participation with educated people. They draw themselves out and it is really harmful. And I think we owe an apology to the third world when the United States and Literature departments want to discuss nonsense.

CA I went to speak to the Teamsters and they were discussing the difficulties in organising people and the declining number of people joining unions and I wanted to ask you whether you thought the unions could ever return to the glory days of the fifties and what would happen to the working people in the future?

CHOMSKY It's not that they're declining, it is that they are being smashed. It started right after the Second World War. It is pretty well documented. Some of the best work done on it was by an Australian, Alex Carey, a good friend of mine. His was kind of disdained and marginalised in Australia because his work was too important for people to pay attention to. Finally, after he died, they started paying attention. He kind of opened up the subject of corporate propaganda and then it was picked up by others. What happened is, during the depression and the Second World War, it was a period of radicalisation of the public all over the world. In Europe the resistance was the first radical democracy, they had workers' control and things like that.

In Europe, that had to be crushed by force. One of the first things the British and the Americans did was what they called 'liberating Europe' and that was to destroy the resistance, particularly targeting the resistance in Italy. Italy probably has been the recipient of more CIA intervention than any other country. They were trying to subvert Italian democracy as it was too radical. But it was the same everywhere. In the United States, which was also pretty radical at the time, they started a major offensive propaganda campaign to try to undermine and destroy unions because that is the main target. Unions were a democratising force. It is not only that they defend workers' rights, they are also a way in which people can get together and pool their limited resources, educate each other and act political. And that is extremely dangerous because few things are hated as much among Western elites as democracy. Democracy is a real threat and they have to bar it somehow or other and unions are a democratising force and so major corporate offences started. The scale is unbelievable—all the way from businesses running programmes in factories where you have captive audiences, forcing workers to study economics—to sports groups, churches, school curriculum.

Right now in Massachusetts—in the most liberal, progressive state in the country in education—I learned a couple a weeks ago from my daughter who lives here, that her son is in a high school in a progressive suburb of Massachusetts which has a curriculum given to them by what is called the objectivist foundation. That's Ayn Rand who indoctrinates people into the belief that altruism is the worst sin: you should be out for yourself and nobody else. They provide curriculum to schools and they teach it. It is shocking, but that is one part of this massive effort to drive out of people's heads the normal human instincts of solidarity, support, sympathy and so on. And the government was at its worst under Reagan. Reagan was a brutal thug, that is why he is so honoured and revered now. He was a murderer abroad—a murderer, a terrorist and killer—and at home he was just a brutal thug. He wanted to destroy the lives of the working people and he was also the most protectionist President in post-war American history—but he was revered with the popular free market. It is all propaganda!

One of the things he did was inform the business world that the government would not apply the laws unorganised. There are laws from the 1930s that give the right to organise and prevent corporations from firing the union organisers. He just basically informed them, 'go ahead and do what you want, we're not going to apply the laws'. By the early nineties you could read in *Business Week* that illegal firing tripled under the Reagan years and to an extent under Clinton (Clinton did it in a different way), and after. It is partially a technique for undermining the union. It makes it possible if union organisers try to organise workers in a factory, for management to put up big signs saying 'transfer operations', meaning that if you organise, you go to Mexico. It is illegal but the government is a criminal government so it doesn't define the laws. It is understandable and the unions are dangerous, they are a democratising force and they also protect workers' rights and that's bad news. The tactics go way back in American history.

Australia has a very powerful labour movement. Back in the 1920s Australians labour leaders visiting the United States were shocked at the repression of American workers. There were hundreds of American workers being murdered by security forces, private or state, into the late thirties when nothing like that was happening in Western Europe or Australia. It's a very repressive and violent labour history and it picked up again after the Second World War in an effort to beat back that democratising social democratic threat. You can see what workers feel about it very easily. Take a look at the unions that now exist. They're predominantly public serviceman and the reason is that in the public sectors the government can't do this, but they can allow the private sector to do it. So there are very high levels of organisation in the public sector unions but not in private sector unions. But can it be reversed? It's kind of hard because this massive propaganda does have affect on people. Kids who are trained under this hideous Ayn Rand propaganda, start to believe it, even the ones who are suffering. So you get an attitude of saying that a guy has a million dollars and I have two cents because he is better than I am, or something like that. It is very possible to beat subservience into people's heads. Perhaps the most striking example of that is the women's movement. Women accepted subordination, beating, abuse, anything—that is the way they thought it was supposed to be. If I had asked my grandmother if she was oppressed, she wouldn't have known what I was talking about, that's the way that the world is, it happened for thousands of years.

The women's movement began as a consciousness raiser. Small groups of women would get together and talk and realise what they had been accepting. Then it changed. It is very different now. If you ask my daughter if she is repressed, she'd laugh. Try to recover, or gauge or hold onto your consciousness, your own instincts; let them come out, into battle. That has to be done before you can revise things. And, of course, it has to be done right with sharp, significant, political changes. The United States is basically a one party state. C. Wright Mill, the great physiologist, fifty years ago, pointed out that there is one party, the business party, and it has two factions. And you can sort of select between the factions. Like in Russia you can pick whether or not you are a member of the communist party. It's not that bad, but it is sort of like that.

There is a huge gap between policy and opinion in the United States; it has been studied carefully. Mainstream political scientists have written about it and it is very striking; they are dealing with crucial issues. Take, say, the main domestic issue—health. The United States has a catastrophic health care system because it is privatised. This means huge inefficiencies and bureaucracies, surveillance, paper work and so on. And the public for decades has wanted to have a national healthcare system. When people are asked in polls, they say they want a health care system like Canada's. The only reason they say Canada's, as it is not a particularly good system, is that no-one can say 'like Australia's' because nobody knows it and Australia's is a far better system. Australia is like on Mars and Canada is right there, you can see it, right against the country.

If you go back to the 2004 election, it was not mentioned. In fact, the *New York Times* had a wonderful article on the previous presidential debate on domestic issues and the *Times* accurately reviewed the debate and pointed out, correctly, that Kerry had never mentioned any government role in health care because it has so little political support—just about three quarters of the population. But they are 'unpeople', is what he meant. What that really meant is that it was posed by the insurance industry and by pharmaceutical corporations and so on, and so they had no political support—so they couldn't mention it. This year it is different, interestingly, and there is good reason for this—it is not that public support has increased—what has happened is that a sector of concentrated capital is now interested. The manufacturing industries are being smashed by health care costs. GM says it costs them 1200 dollars more to produce a car in Detroit than in Windsor, Canada, across the border, because they have a semi-rational health care system. Now they are concerned. Now it has political support because a sector of the manufacturing industry is interested. That is called democracy. I don't know how closely you follow the Australia/US free trade negotiations. They are quite interesting because one of the things that the US was trying to do was destroy the Australian health care system and they partially succeeded. The Australian system was condemned because it had to be evidenced based when they market drugs and the US didn't tolerate that. You have to have a spoken interference with the free market. Corporations have to lie and kill to prove they are right. There was a big attack on the Australian system to try and get it as rotten as the American system and Australia partially conceded on that. I mention health care because in domestic issues that ranks at the top, or close to it, in polls as the most important issue for decades. But it is not politically possible because the 'unpeople' don't count. And it is the same with foreign affairs, for example. And going back to public intellectuals, their role is to make sure that it stays that way.

CA On a totally different note, I came through Las Vegas and it is an incredible place, really interesting. It is full of working class people and yet it seems to be beneath the contempt of academics who talk about Las Vegas in a derogatory way. Given that it is the fastest growing city in America, what does that say about America?

CHOMSKY When our kids were little we used to go to a little restaurant nearby that was inexpensive and we knew all the waitresses and so on—you know, working people. These people who worked there, they weren't impoverished but they would get together, save money and go to Las Vegas and blow all their money on the casinos. This was of their dreams; what they did once a year. These are ways of ripping off workers and the government is involved in it directly. Massachusetts has a state lottery. State lottery is simply a way of cheating people, it's a way of developing a regressive tax system. It's been studied, but it is pretty obvious, if you look at the communities where people buy lottery tickets that it's inversely related to the level of education. And the reason is obvious, if you think about it when you buy a lottery ticket you are throwing away your money, otherwise the state wouldn't run them. It is the same in Las Vegas. But poor people, partly out of desperation, think 'maybe I'll be like that guy on television who won a million dollars and what do I have to lose, my life is ruined anyway?'

I've watched people come in and they have schemes. It's like being drilled in Ayn Rand or groupist fanaticism; it is simply a way of ripping people off. I don't think it should be illegal. I think it is illegal for the state to do it, the state should not be involved in robbing people—but if the waitresses at the restaurant want to blow their money in Las Vegas, that is their choice. If they ask me what I think, I'd tell them that they are crazy. There are better things you can do with your money and you can have more fun. And they are victims, they are victims of a propaganda system which it glorifies. Take a look at TV shows set in Las Vegas. It looks smart. Take Cuba, sooner or later the US is going to turn Cuba back into a colony as it was throughout its history until 1959 and the way I think they will do it is through television. The young people in Cuba, and in the third world, watch Hollywood television programmes. And if you look at any Hollywood television programmes it depicts a life in which people have no problems. The only problem you have is perhaps a problem with your girlfriend. But you don't have a job, you don't work, you're rich. And a kid in Cuba is going to look at that and say, 'why can't I live like that?' He thinks about what his parents lived like, he thinks, 'I want to live like that [depiction of life in Hollywood films] too.' And you can see that here, too. The poor people who watch this stuff think, 'I don't live like this so it must be my fault.' These are hard things to break.

Take the election. The elections are basically run by the public relations industry—the same industry that sells toothpaste and lifestyle drugs on television. And they do it the same way. When you look at an ad on television, you don't expect to learn anything. If we had anything remotely like a free market General Motors would put up an ad in which they'd say, 'here is my product, here are its characteristics'—thirty seconds and get informed. That would be creating informed consumers making rational choices. But they don't want that, they want uniformed consumers making irrational choices for the purpose of advertising, to undermine markets. You can undermine democracy in the same way. You don't want people voting on the basis of issues, that is one reason for the big disparity between people and policies. You want them to vote on the basis of image and poor quality.

Barack Obama is good looking, and he looks you straight in the eye—you can trust him. Hillary Clinton shed a tear in New Hampshire to be more feminine and win people over. George Bush created an image of the kind of guy you'd like to meet in a bar, but he has to get back to the ranch. I am convinced—I can't prove it—that he is taught to mispronounce words, that he was taught to say 'misunderestimated'. He didn't say things like that at Yale, I'm pretty sure. But I think he is probably taught to do that and it makes sense because then the liberal intellectuals will ridicule him and they write books about Bush's mispronunciations. And then strategists consider the population and say, 'it is easy for the world elitists who are drinking French wine and eating feasts, ridiculing ordinary guys like us—like George Bush and you—just ordinary guys who want to have a drink at the bar. We have to get rid of these bourgeois elitists.' Meanwhile they go and kick them [these ordinary guys] in the face.

But that is the way you undermine democracy, if you watch the campaigns.

Photo credits

Harold Bloom: Michael Marsland

Noam Chomsky: Donna Coveney

Jim Cullen: Cynthia Nixon

Dana Gioia: none given

Todd Gitlin: Jill Krementz

James Green: none given

Stephen Greenblatt: Jürgen Bauer

Kenneth Jackson: Lisa Keller

Paul Kane: Philip Perkis

Camille Paglia: Misa Martin

Howard Zinn: Robert Birnbaum